Wide-Area Networks
In Libraries

Supplements to Computers in Libraries

Wide-Area Networks in Libraries:

Technology, Applications, and Trends

Edited by Gregory Zuck
and Bruce Flanders

Meckler
Westport • London

Library of Congress Cataloging-in-Publication Data

Wide-area networks in libraries: technology, applications, and trends
/ edited by Gregory Zuck and Bruce Flanders.
    p. cm.--(Supplements to Computers in libraries; 58)
    Includes bibliographical references and index.
    ISBN 0-88736-841-7 : $
    1. Wide area networks (Computer networks)--Library applications.
2. Reference services (Libraries)--Automation. 3. Information
technology. 4. Libraries--Automation. I. Zuck, Gregory James.
II. Flanders, Bruce L. III. Series.
Z678.93.W53W53   1992
021.6'5--dc20   92-41407
                                                            CIP

British Library Cataloguing-in-Publication Data

Zuck, Gregory
    Wide Area Networks in Libraries:
    Technology, Applications, and Trends.-
    (Supplements to Computers in Libraries
    Series)
    I. Title II. Flanders, Bruce III. Series
    004.6

    ISBN 0-88736-841-7

Meckler Publishing, the publishing division of Meckler Corporation,
    11 Ferry Lane West, Westport, CT 06880.
Meckler Ltd., Artillery House, Artillery Row, London SW1P 1RT, U.K.

Printed on acid free paper.
Printed and bound in the United States of America.

Dedicated to:

Essie Sappenfield
Friend, wife, lover, and inspiration
G. Z.

* * * * * *

Thanks to my supportive wife, Karen, and to my entire family
B. F.

Contents

Introduction—WANs in Libraries: Technology, Applications, and Trends

Gregory Zuck, Ph.D., Library Director
Southwestern College

The approach of this introductory chapter is threefold: to introduce the reader to wide-area networking (WAN) technology, to describe WAN applications, and to point out major trends.

First, wide-area networks will be described in terms of their basic technology. What makes up a WAN? What software, hardware, and telecommunications requirements and options are there? What is the meaning of the many acronyms found in the networking literature? What about the confusing array of protocols and standards? I propose to describe the "parts and pieces" that make up a wide-area network. You will not read detailed information about the seven layers of the Open System Interconnection (OSI) model nor learn of every commercial product or protocol.

Second, actual and potential applications of wide-area networks in libraries will be described from the perspective of small, local WANs as well as a state-wide or regional network, emphasizing the varieties of network capabilities, the technology, and supporting equipment. Much can be done with little in cost and hardware.

Third will be an introduction to the national and international networks that are much discussed in the library literature. What is the current and future status and potential of such networks as BITNET (CREN) and Internet using the Transmission Control Protocol/Internet Protocol (TCP/IP) and the promise of the International Standards Organization (ISO) protocol named Open System Interconnection (OSI)? Libraries of all sizes and types will be greatly influenced by the trends in WAN networks. The directions state and federal governments are taking to encourage information transfer, telecommunications industry trends, and advances in computer technology have implications for small school libraries as well as for large academic, research, and specialized libraries.

Definitions

Telecommunications networks are often defined by the size of the geographical area they encompass. Local-area networks (LANs) are two or more computers, very often personal computers, that are connected in order to share information within a limited physical space. A LAN is often a cluster of PCs that are in the same room, floor, or building. They may be able to access and use the information found in spreadsheets, database files, and written reports. Often the LANs allow the sharing of laser printers, faxes, and other hardware and software. LAN interconnections may span several miles within a complex of buildings such as an academic campus or an industrial site. Recent reports suggest that LANs have entered ninety-eight percent of the larger U.S. companies, in which as many as forty percent of their PCs are connected. Using personal computers in a campus-wide network environment, many academic libraries provide access to library resources such as CD-ROM databases and online catalogs to classrooms, faculty offices, and dormitories. A campus-wide network with electronic mail capability can allow patrons to reserve and check out books. Interlibrary loans and other messages and transactions can be initiated from outside the library building.

A wide-area network (WAN) is a network of computers, often PCs in the library setting, that cover a very large geographical area. The wide-area network uses long-distance communications such as regular phone lines, leased lines, a packet-switched network, like Tymnet, and even satellite communications. Distances may vary from a few miles to networks spanning states, regions, and ultimately, the globe. The WAN shares many of the same characteristics and processes of a LAN since the sharing of information is the primary objective. Information traveling on a WAN traditionally is comprised of text and binary files. More recently, audio and video information is available through WANs. Given sufficient bandwidth, WANs can support interactive videoconferencing.

A possible WAN is illustrated in Figure 1. This network's topology is star-shaped; the design resembles a central hub with radiating spokes or arms. The entire system could be comprised of personal computers. A PC, in theory, could serve as the central hub, called the network file server. In one of the book's case study chapters, such a PC-based WAN delivers electronic mail (e-mail) as a means of routing interlibrary loan requests and responses. Each remote library on the network maintains a computer with a modem which connects to the central file server via regular phone lines. At a set time, each of the remote computers is polled, and interlibrary loan transactions and other messages are transferred to the appropriate recipients on the network. This wide-area network is inexpensive and efficient. With a modest expenditure much can be done and done well.

A second WAN design, as shown in Figure 2, offers greater possibilities. Naturally this network is more expensive to equip and operate.

Each library in System A and System B could have interconnected LANs at the building, campus, or regional level. The networks could be LAN to WAN and/or WAN to WAN. A network of this sophistication, in which

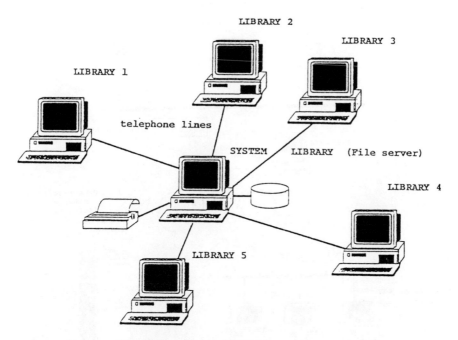

Figure 1. A possible WAN configuration.

multiple networks are linked (internetworked), requires a higher level of networking skill, and greater coordination among participating agencies.

Two additional network configurations are emerging. Metropolitan-area networks (MANs) are installed in many major cities in the United States. MANs often cover a radius of five to fifty miles. Fiber-optic and coaxial lines are typically employed to connect buildings and facilities. Fiber-optic material is considerably more expensive to install, nonetheless, telecommunications companies are in fierce competition to "wire" major downtown business districts. Three notable advantages of fiber-optic lines are: (1) very high communications speeds, (2) no loss of data, and (3) the capacity to carry more data. The enterprise network is another network configuration that was once considered a rarity, but is now gaining acceptance. The "enterprise" is the (often geographically dispersed) company or institution with a wide variety of computer resources and data—linked in an "enterprise-wide" network. As the parts and pieces to construct and run networks become cheaper, easier to install and manage, and as standardization increases, individual companies will

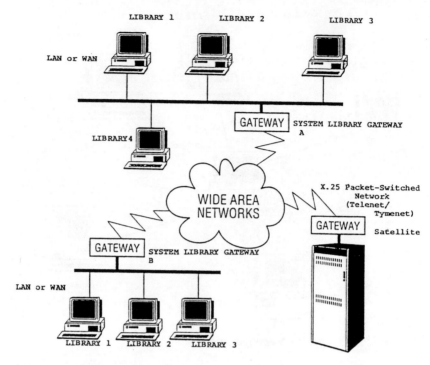

Figure 2. Another possible WAN configuration.

build their own networks linking their geographically separated facilities. Enterprise networks can be WANs tied to LANs and can be found within a city, state, or region—or spanning the globe.

Parts and Pieces

WANs transfer information along physical communications highways. Whether the highways are common twisted-pair telephone lines, or etherial highways linked by satellite or line-of-sight microwave dishes, there is electronic hardware and software that interprets and routes the information. Knowledge of the physical links of WANs and LANs must include an understanding of such data communications terms as repeaters, bridges, routers, brouters, and gateways.

A repeater is a piece of telecom hardware that amplifies data signals. Its purpose is to extend the sending range of the signal by boosting its strength at periodic distances. For example, a network may be able to send data only down 100 yards of cable before the signal is weakened. Adding a repeater at that point regenerates the signals for another 100 yards, without losing signal quality.

A bridge is a device, much like a VCR in shape and general appearance, that acts as a traffic cop between various networks or subcomponents of networks. Bridges are used to keep network traffic within the localized network, and to allow only appropriate messages to travel to or from that local network.

Routers are like bridges, but add capabilities to intelligently route data to the correct network address. The telephone system uses routers to direct data to a four-part address code consisting of country + area + central office + four-digit line number. A WAN router is protocol dependent.

LAN to WAN interconnections require bridges and/or routers. While this equipment is relatively expensive, the cost of communications hardware appears to be decreasing.

Brouters, as the name indicates, mix bridge and router technologies. Brouters process internetworking connections quickly, acting like a bridge, and can handle communications among networks with different protocols.

Gateways are hardware devices and related software applications that connect networks, whether LAN to LAN, LAN to WAN, or WAN to WAN, that have dissimilar protocols. A gateway represents the most sophisticated interconnection process and is used to connect not only private networks, but commercial Public Data Networks (PDNs), such as Tymnet, Telenet, CompuServe, and Sprintnet.

Each one of these devices oversees the transfer of data from one computer or network to another. They operate at different levels of the International Standards Organization (ISO) networking model: the Open Systems Interconnection (OSI) model. The telecom industry is slowly migrating toward adoption of this model. Implementation of the OSI model promotes the advancement of telecommunications by establishing a common standard agreed upon by all interested commercial firms and government bodies. The OSI model uses layers, which, from the simplest to the most complex, are the physical, data link, network, transport, session, presentation, and application. The lowest layer deals with the physical aspect of cables and connectors and the highest level concerns common agreement in such areas as the transfer of files and electronic mail messages, or the ability to transparently search OPACs of different vendors whose systems are running on disparate hardware platforms.

Another important aspect of WAN data communications technology is the transmission lines. (Once again, the use of acronyms in the WAN literature is profuse. The meaning and implications of circuit and packet networks, T-1, FT-1, T-3, Digital Data Service [DDS], and Public Data Networks [PDNs] will make your readings of WAN literature more understandable and productive.)

Circuit switching is the manner in which telephone systems are traditionally linked. Telephonic voice messages are sent in analog form from one circuit to another at a speed of approximately 9,600 bits to 64,000 bits per second. With the continuing growth of computer networking and advances in communications technology, three important changes have occurred.

First, much of the computerized information now moves in a packet-switching mode. Unsequenced packets, chunks of data, are sent in fast bursts between computer nodes on the network. At the front of each packet, information is included that identifies the receiving network or computer, and the manner in which packets should be sequenced when received at the recipient site. Packet switching also permits the storing and rerouting of the data packets. Second, data is now packaged in digital form. Computers communicate internally and externally in the digital format. Digital transmissions are much faster and contain fewer errors than voice (analog) format when transmitted via standard telephone lines. Third, transmission bandwidth measured in millions of bits per second (mbps) is becoming more feasible. Multimedia transmissions of voice, motion, and images in very high resolution (digitized video) are new demands that require great speeds and bandwidths.

References to T-1 are often found in the literature on WANs and telecommunications networking. The T communications system is a product of long-distance telephone carriers, such as Bell Telephone, US Sprint, or MCI. It is digital, operates at bandwidths between 56kbps (kilobits per second) and 1.544mbps (or higher), and can carry voice, video, and data. A T-1 circuit-switched system is the communications backbone of many commercial WANs. A T-3 network performs at even greater speeds (45mbps). The backbone of the National Science Foundation network (NSFnet) is T-3. Needless to say, T1 and T3 telecom technologies are expensive. In 1988, Fractional T-1 (FT-1) was offered at a lower lease rate, offering the use of a portion of the total bandwidth. World-wide competition, technological innovations, and the drop in the manufacturing of telecommunications components will contribute to reductions in the cost of T networks as WAN backbones.

The highly competitive long-distance telephone companies are referred to as Public Data Networks (PDNs) or Value-Added Networks (VANs). All are packet-switched networks that offer volume discounts for high-volume users. Three additional PDNs familiar to librarians are Tymnet, CompuServe, and Datapac of Telecom Canada.

In the United States, the divestiture of the Bell Telephone System in the 1980s introduced competitive incentives for the traditional long-distance carriers. Private networks quickly offered their own digital data services (DDSs) on T-1 lines.

Fiber-optic networks are even more impressive in their capabilities. Fiber Distributed Data Interface (FDDI), a network standard promulgated by the American National Standards Institute (ANSI), is a 100mbps design for LANs and MANs. Very large files, databases, and video imaging require such capacity. Many experts in the telecom field believe that FDDI is the backbone option of choice.

At present, most libraries use the modem for PC-based communications. Transmission speeds of 2,400 to 9,600bps are common. When digital data services (DDSs) are employed, modems as the interface with the network are replaced by a Data Service Unit/Channel Service Unit (DSU/CSU). These hardware interfaces allow a direct, digital, high-quality connection to network lines (digital) at transmission rates of 64kbps to 565mbps. Error correction assures that even at these speeds data arrives error free.

Trends

X.25 is the current international WAN digital telecommunications protocol. Any two computers in the world, PCs or mainframe, can communicate with each other by connecting through a public or private X.25 packet-switching network. Error checking is a strong point of the protocol, however, as each packet is checked for errors at each switch on the network, packet-switched networks are comparatively slow. Transmission speeds at approximately 56kbps within the dedicated packet-switch network level, and as slow as 19.6kbps at the packet assembler disassembler (PAD) are typical. By comparison, within and among Ethernet-based LANs the speed is near 2.5mbps, and interconnects using fiber-optic cable support transmission rates reaching 100mbps.

Integrated Services Digital Network (ISDN) is a proposed international wide-area standard to replace X.25. Some experts predict that ISDN will become *the* data communications standard, and will ultimately supplant current telephone system technology on a wide scale. ISDN is an all digital system that can put voice, data, fax, and video communications on one major, public network. Transmission rates of 144kbps to 2mbps and the promise of economically attractive installation costs may well propel ISDN into the mainstream. The emerging standard in the United States is National ISDN 1, although a perplexing proliferation of ISDN standards continues to thwart its adoption.

Just as ISDN is beginning to gain recognition and momentum as the new standard for wide-area network communications, frame relay has appeared as a strong rival for the same market. Frame relay derives its name from its method of efficiently relaying "frames" of information (blocks of data of varying lengths) across a packet-switched network. As a WAN service, frame relay will offer higher transmission speeds (64kbps to 1.5mbps) with considerable reduction in private-line and local access costs. Broad connectivity between existing computer and telecommunications equipment (bridges and routers) is possible. Of the big three U.S. long-distance carriers (AT&T, MCI, and US Sprint), Sprint is implementing frame relay technology most aggressively. Frame relay is predicted to be the dominant WAN network model until 1995.

By the mid-1990s a breakthrough is envisioned with the advent of two nascent, competing networks: Switched Multimegabit Data Service (SMDS) and Asynchronous Transfer Mode (ATM). Both SMDS and ATM will send information in the form of a "cell relay," containing a fixed length of 53 bytes of data. Both SMDS and ATM will be based on the metropolitan-area network (MAN) 802.6 Institute of Electrical and Electronic Engineers (IEEE) standard.

SMDS still uses the packet-switched network mode and will boast speeds of 1.5mbps to 45mbps. ATM will be a true cell relay model reaching transmission speeds of 45mbps to 600mbps. ATM is considered a fundamental rethinking of LAN/WAN interface technology that can accommodate real multimedia networking. Multi-gigabit speeds are demanded by multimedia traffic, because it will contain vast amounts of information. The Consultative Committee on International Telegraph and Telephone (CCITT) and ANSI have adopted the ATM standard.

One more "X-dot" CCITT standard needs to be described when discussing WANs. X.400 is an international standard that defines the format of e-mail addressing. Major telephone carriers, for example, AT&T, Sprint, MCI, and Easy Link, offer the X.400 standard for message systems that serve world-wide markets.

In 1969 a packet-switched network system was funded by the U.S. Department of Advanced Research Projects Agency (DARPA). The network was dubbed ARPANET. It connected minicomputers with dedicated 56kbps telephone lines. ARPANET is the true progenitor of today's WAN. In 1981, BITNET (Because It's Time Network) was instituted. Currently over 2,300 members belong to BITNET—many of which are colleges and universities, and their libraries. The major tenet behind BITNET was the need for the free flow of information among noncommercial institutions and research centers. The network includes institutions in all major parts of the world, including Japan, England, Central America, the Middle East, and Europe.

In September 1989 BITNET merged with CSNET and was renamed The Corporation for Research and Educational Networking (CREN), managed by EDUCOM, a nonprofit higher education consortium. Most of the BITNET communications are in the form of e-mail messages and transferred files that travel on leased lines. Over 1,000 institutions in the United States are members.

The latest and hottest network concept, obviously, is the Internet—a network of networks. Millions of users in dozens of countries, using hundreds of thousands of computers, are tapped into the Internet. Computer resources linked to the Internet vary widely, but the common bond is the Transmission Control Protocol/Internet Protocol (TCP/IP) protocol suite. TCP/IP is a suite of communications protocols standardized by the U.S. Department of Defense. Until the Open Systems Interconnection (OSI) model becomes more accepted and widely implemented, TCP/IP will continue to be the de facto standard for multivendor internetworking.

At this time (1992), the Internet is still predominantly an e-mail and file transfer system linking colleagues in educational and research institutions. The Internet is being used increasingly, however, for access to remote databases, including library resources. Since the Internet allows networks using all kinds of hardware and software configurations to interconnect easily, many automated library systems and online public catalogs (OPACs) are implementing TCP/IP access to their resources. In the United States, the NSFnet is being replaced by the federally-funded National Research and Education Network (NREN). President George Bush signed a NREN bill (S.272, the High Performance Computing Act which became PL 102-194) on December 9, 1991. This new law authorizes $2.9 billion to be spent over the next five years. The management of this network of networks continues to be in the purview of the National Science Foundation (NSF). A major portion of NREN funding will facilitate the linking of research and educational institutions, and commercial interests to the network. The American Library Association has been very active and supportive of this new electronic highway system.

New standards and protocols will emerge in the next few years. For example, the Multipurpose Internet Mail Extensions (MIME) standard will address the need to transfer multimedia data in addition to traditional text and binary files.

The future of WANs in libraries is very promising. But today's examples of WAN library applications are equally exciting. Innovative librarians can take advantage of recent technological advances to leapfrog over traditional limitations in transmission speed and hardware expense. With continued technological breakthroughs, more attractive cost/performance ratios are sure to attract the attention of school and public libraries. As we learn more about WANs and their potential, we become better able to exploit them to improve library service. And, improved client service, after all, is the reason we implement WANs and other technologies in our libraries.

KICNET: A Microcomputer-Based State-Wide Library WAN

Bruce Flanders, Director of Technology
Kansas State Library

Abstract

KICNET is a personal computer-based wide-area network linking 150 public, academic, medical, and school libraries in a state-wide interlibrary loan telecommunications system. KICNET is an example of a low-cost WAN application that nonetheless has had a significant impact on library services. KIC-NET, administered by the Kansas State Library, is a store-and-forward network using commercial e-mail software to reliably and promptly deliver nearly 600,000 messages each year. Recent enhancements to the network have extended its capabilities without substantial network administration requirements or added cost.

Introduction

While most of the chapters in this book describe complex wide-area networks supported by minicomputer or mainframe hardware platforms, WANs do not necessarily imply major commitments of hardware resources or finances. In Kansas, a low-cost WAN has been in operation for over two years to serve a vital library resource sharing function. Overall state expenses for the entire duration of this project, including the purchase of network server hardware, software, 100 copies of remote user software, and all long-distance telecommunications support for 150 libraries, from late 1989 to early 1992, has amounted to less than $70,000. That is a small sum indeed for what has developed into a mission-critical service provided by the Kansas State Library for its constituent libraries. It proves that given creative management and well-designed personal computer-based applications, effective library WANs serving focused communities and functions need not be mega-dollar propositions.

Fast and reliable interlibrary loan telecommunications have been made possible in Kansas through KICNET (Kansas Interlibrary Communications Network), a private electronic mail wide-area network administered by the Kansas State Library. Its purpose is to provide libraries with an inexpensive, fast, and reliable means for transmitting interlibrary loan requests and responses. It has proven to be significantly less expensive than OCLC Interlibrary Loan, yet it provides approximately the same speed of delivery, and an obvious advantage over sending requests and responses by U.S. mail. It has not supplanted the use of the OCLC Interlibrary Loan Subsystem among larger public, and particularly, academic libraries in the state, but has proven to be an efficient and effective interlibrary loan tool for smaller libraries who had previously used non-electronic means for their resource-sharing communications. These smaller libraries in Kansas can now, with the advent of Auto-Graphics/OCLC's SharePAC CD-ROM-based union catalog product, transmit interlibrary loan requests to OCLC full member institutions via SharePAC's link to the OCLC Interlibrary Loan Subsystem.

KICNET is the first fully successful WAN interlibrary loan system implemented in Kansas to augment OCLC Interlibrary Loan, and to provide an affordable ILL solution for smaller libraries in the state.[1] Prior to KICNET's implementation in 1989, four successive networks, the first two of which were "home-grown," attempted to address the interlibrary loan needs of smaller libraries. Both PROFS, the state government's electronic mail network, and ALANET, ALA's electronic mail network that ceased operation in early 1992, were also used for a time. None of these first four systems proved satisfactory; the home-grown systems were buggy and unreliable, PROFS was too awkward to use from remote dial-in sites, and ALANET was too expensive.

Background Research

KICNET's current configuration was reached after extensive study. A study team was formed in early 1989 to put an end (hopefully) to the revolving door process of failed telecommunications systems. First, a national survey of interlibrary loan networks was conducted.[2] Unfortunately, it yielded no significant revelations. We found that few states have a formal state-wide interlibrary loan network; rather, most employ a mixture of systems, almost always including OCLC, telefacsimile (fax), and mailed forms. Nearly every state reported that they were generally satisfied with their current arrangement, but that they were actively looking for alternatives. As a follow-up to the survey, a cost, functionality, and performance evaluation of interlibrary loan network alternatives was made. We determined that OCLC Group Access Capability (GAC) was the most highly developed and most desirable system, but it was also the most costly approach. Fax, PROFS (IBM's mainframe-based e-mail program available through the state government computer center), AT&T Mail, MCI Mail, and ALANET were also examined.[3]

In the final analysis, private e-mail systems appeared to display the highest degree of functionality for the cost. A private e-mail network is just that—an e-mail network established and administered for a specific clientele.

There is really no substantive difference between our network, KICNET, and a large network such as ALANET or MCI Mail. Ours is obviously smaller in scope, serving (currently) only the state of Kansas, but in terms of its ability to store and forward messages, it matches, and in certain areas, exceeds the functionality of its larger brethren. By choosing to run one's own e-mail system, network administration became an obvious overhead consideration, but as a tradeoff, we could design the network to more precisely match our requirements and keep costs low—a goal that, as it turns out, we were able to accomplish with amazing effectiveness.

cc:Mail Software Chosen

We examined a number of commercially-available e-mail packages and settled on cc:Mail. cc:Mail, Inc., which in 1991 became a division of Lotus Development Corporation, is the third fastest growing software company in the United States. The size and success of the software firm was an important consideration in our decision to implement a cc:Mail-based network; after so many attempts to establish a network, we wished to make a sound, conservative choice of supporting software. cc:Mail appeared to be an ideal solution from a technical point of view: it accommodates the installation of a central "post office" (mail router) on a stand-alone PC using the cc:Mail LAN Package, and provides access to remote sites via a software module called cc:Mail Remote. All of the Kansas libraries on the network could send mail to each other via voice-grade telephone lines by asynchronous communications with the central post office. This appeared to be an extremely easy-to-use solution with minimal administrative overhead. It is, by the way, a classic "store-and-forward" network topology.

cc:Mail, which has been shipping since October 1985, is used by many corporations, such as Boeing and Security Pacific Bank, by governmental agencies, such as the Social Security Administration, the U.S. Department of Energy, the California Department of Forestry, and universities, such as the University of California and the University of Illinois. cc:Mail has over one million users in over 5,000 networks, and has captured thirty-five percent of the international e-mail market share. It operates in DOS, Windows, OS/2, and Macintosh environments, and can support simple six-user LANs, all the way up to enterprise-wide networks with hundreds of thousands of messages, tens of thousands of users, and dozens of servers. cc:Mail supports links to other electronic mail systems, such as IBM's PROFS and DISOSS, DEC VAX/VMS mail and All-in-1, Western Union's EasyLink and Telex, CompuServe's InfoPlex, MCI Mail, UNIX's SMTP and UUCP, and Telemail.

cc:Mail appeared to be perfect for us, since it readily supported the necessary WAN configuration. We did, by the way, find other software packages that had roughly the same feature set as cc:Mail, but none that provided a gateway capability to PROFS—a function mandated by our state government computer center.

The Kansas State Library implemented cc:Mail on a test basis at ten libraries in August and September 1989. These libraries reported favorably concerning the speed, ease of earning, and ease of use of the software. The state-wide interlibrary loan user's council, at an October 1989 meeting, voted unanimously to give its formal approval to this new system, which we dubbed KICNET. Training began in earnest in late October. By year's end, 75 libraries were up and running.

Network Design

In its administration of KICNET, the Kansas State Library operates a network "file server," which is a personal computer/modem workstation that acts as a central hub for the network, storing messages for libraries until it next calls them to upload and download interlibrary loan messages. File server "gateway" software telecommunicates to all participants at preset times. It does this automatically, keeping track of the time with the computer's internal clock. E-mail calls are initiated to libraries around the state at preset times each hour, 24 hours a day, 7 days a week. We have reserved two half-hour periods for occasions when we need to manually call a library that has missed its call, and for weekly database maintenance work. Frequently, that slack time is unused. The network is purposely designed so that all calls emanate from the State Library, thus centralizing long-distance expenses. Remote nodes, or libraries participating in the network, make sure that at a predetermined time their computer is on, the KICNET software is placed in the "waiting for call" mode, the modem is on and attached to a phone line. Many calls are scheduled during evening and night hours; KICNET accommodates unattended calling. In fact, many libraries prefer the call to come in at night—particularly those libraries which have only one phone line. These unattended communications sessions are reliable because the remote node software rejects voice calls and non-KICNET modem-based calls, and resets itself to receive the call from the cc:Mail post office.

Numerous libraries with a single telephone line also have a fax machine, and employ a fax/modem/phone "manager"—an intelligent switch box costing approximately $250 to reliably and automatically route calls to the appropriate device. Most libraries using a shared line for KICNET and their fax machine simply unplug one device while using the other. This arrangement is simple and cheap, but it is also inconvenient, since one can easily forget to connect the fax after using the modem. Other libraries simply employ a manual A-B switch. This is somewhat more convenient, but still requires operators to remember to flip the switch. Automatic switch managers have proven to be reliable once set up correctly, and they are the recommended solution to the problem of shared phone lines.

A password is required to load KICNET software and to establish communications sessions. (As a matter of convenience, the password and other software "switches" are included in a batch file that loads the software on each participant's computer.) All messages and message transmissions are encrypted to inhibit unauthorized examination. A sophisticated data compression scheme is used to minimize to the size of KICNET messages and speed message transfer, thereby reducing transmission charges. Also, all message transmissions utilize an X.PC error-correction protocol to ensure message and file integrity.

The Kansas State Library is able to keep the list of participants current at all remote nodes by issuing an automatic directory update transaction. It is sent to remote users like a regular message, but is interpreted by KICNET software as a directory update. This is an elegant solution to an ongoing maintenance task.

Each morning a staff member backs up the KICNET message database, then runs a "network traffic" statistical report. At least once a week, we run database integrity checks, pack the database, and de-fragment the hard disk, all important steps in keeping the file server "tuned" for the fastest possible response. Less than 30 minutes is required to perform all utility functions.

One administrative overhead detail that is time-consuming and aggravating is manually polling libraries that missed their calls. At the beginning of the network's operation, the State Library decided to poll libraries again if they miss their calls (for whatever reason—hardware problem, operator error, telephone line glitch). Two half-hour periods reserved for such a function are sometimes quite busy.

Network Costs

Costs for operating the network have been extremely reasonable. "Post office" software costs $1,500, and remote user software costs $100 each for 150 remote sites.

Telecommunications costs have actually been lower than projected. The Kansas State Library calls out over the state's telecommunications network, KANS-A-N, which offers an approximate cost savings of 45 percent for long-distance calls, as compared to commercial long-distance carriers.

Telecommunications costs for 150 libraries averages $2,000 per month, or $24,000 annually (see Figure 1). Software maintenance contracts cost $50 per remote user per year, so with a 150-library network, the cost is $7,500 annually. Software maintenance contracts entitle users to unlimited technical support and free software upgrades during the year.

The file server software accommodates the automatic creation and maintenance of a calling log. This is a file that contains information concerning every call, including the number of messages transmitted. This has proven to be invaluable in evaluating both the performance and the utilization of the network. KICNET is currently handling an average of 1,600 transmitted messages daily for 150 libraries. This translates to 584,000 transmitted messages annually. Thus, each message is transmitted for approximately $0.05. KICNET has proven to be amazingly economical to operate.

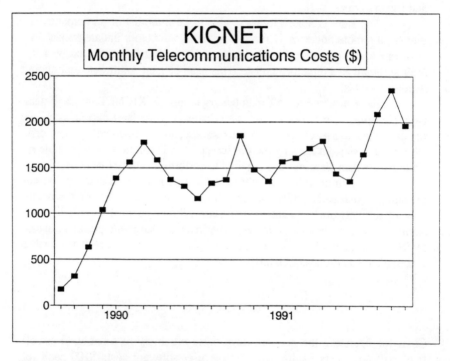

Figure 1. Telecommunications costs.

User Training

Libraries have appreciated KICNET's ease of learning and ease of use. cc:Mail software is menu-driven, and is so intuitive that documentation is almost superfluous. Online context-sensitive help screens provide immediate explanations of program functions. Additionally, the Kansas State Library has created a two-page KICNET Quick Reference Guide which serves as system documentation. Only a few of our users (typically the "computer junkies") have ever cracked the overwhelmingly thick and comprehensive cc:Mail manual. Libraries can press a few keys to call book, photocopy, reference question, or interlibrary loan statistics templates up from disk storage, and complete them with information relating to the requested material. Responses to requests are returned via the system; turnaround time is typically two days.

We have found that cc:Mail's menu-driven user interface accommodates users from the least to the most sophisticated. The menus are arranged so only active functions related to the user's current activity can be selected. The most often-used choice is always highlighted first to make it easier for novices to complete an electronic mail sequence. Single key selections allow expert users to quickly move through more advanced features. cc:Mail is "modeless," that is, users can edit messages, create new file folders, change a distribution list, or whatever, at any point in cc:Mail—no preplanning is required.

cc:Mail messages are created using a built-in full-screen text editor supporting word processing block operations, including insert and delete, search and replace, word wrap, tabs, and margins. Interlibrary loan borrow and photocopy request templates, as well as reference query and interlibrary loan statistics reporting form templates are supplied to remote users (complete with their return mailing address) for ease of use of the system and for achieving greater consistency in the formatting of interlibrary loan messages.

cc:Mail is organized around common paper-based mail terms so that it will be immediately familiar to the user. Messages are received in an "in box," and may be filed in private folders. A public mail directory, much like a telephone book, allows users to easily select destinations for the messages. The creation and maintenance of distribution lists for mass mailings is readily accomplished, as is the sending of "certified mail" that verifies message receipt.

KICNET software provides file folders to organize and store messages. A recent survey of KICNET libraries indicates that 55 percent of the participants use these folders to maintain copies of incoming and outbound messages. Of this 55 percent, the majority also maintain copies of requests in hard copy printouts. Old habits are hard to break! Most libraries maintain separate folders for incoming messages, outbound messages, and administrative messages. Some libraries maintain additional folders containing interlibrary loan statistical data, and filled photocopy borrowing requests, which has proven to be an easy way to keep copyright compliance information.

cc:Mail allows users to act on messages individually or by groups. Users can create, read, reply, forward, print, move, or copy to folders, and delete messages one by one, or by groups. It is useful to interlibrary loan librarians to mark all of the new incoming messages and to print them all en masse. Users can use database search tools such as name, keyword phrase, and calendar date to work on the messages of their choice.

KICNET participants range from high school libraries in small, rural communities to some major university libraries, with broad representation of public, academic, and community college libraries. Multitype representation from each regional library system is strong. Training all of these libraries was a formidable task.

Network Growth

In attempting to intelligently expand KICNET, the Kansas State Library has examined the composition of the current network. An obvious low-participation area was school libraries, a group which the State Library is committed to increasingly involve in the state-wide library networking environment. As a result of this study, it was decided to provide grants to purchase cc:Mail software for several school libraries that were former recipients of on-line database searching grants. These are prime candidates for enhanced interlibrary loan request capability, since they are generating more borrowing requests as a result of their on-line searching.

The administrative load of implementing the network was initially quite heavy. (This lessened dramatically after all participants were trained.) My assistant and I spent over half of our time during the latter part of 1989 in training library staff, providing technical support, and maintaining the network file server and its all-important database.

We decided to train each library on an individual basis; to make "house calls." This was the preferred approach for two reasons: (1) it provided librarians with a chance to interact with us and obtain individualized attention, and (2) it allowed us to test the software at each location. We found significant variance in personal computer/modem configurations, and often software profile changes and/or hardware switch setting changes were required to accommodate KICNET communications.

KICNET growth was initially explosive, and has since tapered off to a slow, manageable rate (see Figure 2). No KICNET library, once on the network, has chosen to drop off.

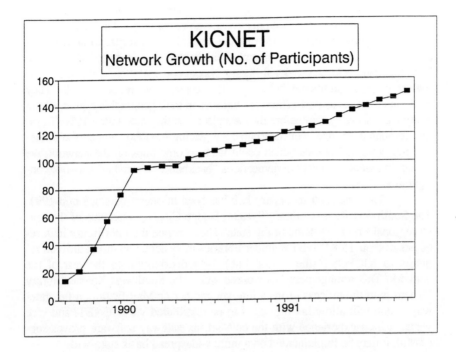

Figure 2. Network growth.

Participation in KICNET is open to any Kansas library that enters its current acquisitions into the state-wide union catalog, the Kansas Library Catalog (KLC), the 2.5 million title union database which is produced, incidentally, in both microfiche and CD-ROM format. Local hardware requirements for KICNET include an IBM or compatible personal computer, 384K RAM, hard disk, 2,400bps or 9,600bps modem, and printer. (A Macintosh version of the remote user software is scheduled to ship in 1992.) cc:Mail software costs $295 ($225, governmental agencies), or less in large quantity. As mentioned earlier, the State Library assumes all long-distance costs for the network, thus making KICNET incredibly economical. The optimal file server for a network of our size is an 80386-based personal computer.

Strategic Plan for KICNET

Telecommunications have recently been enhanced by the installation of 9,600bps modems for the Kansas State Library and the two highest volume KICNET participants.

The implementation of high-speed modems in KICNET points to the future of the network. It is not only conceivable, but likely that KICNET will continue to grow at such a pace that the single hub (post office) network topology will be outgrown. Fortunately, cc:Mail has the ability to link multiple hubs together. With the regional library system configuration in the state, it is logical to place additional hubs at system centers, wherever possible. They could in effect act as post offices for libraries in their geographic region, filling many requests in-system before they are placed on the state-wide KICNET system through a "bridge" between hubs. By placing 9,600bps modems at strategic high-volume libraries which could later become hubs on the network, we create, in essence, a telecommunications "backbone," a standard network configuration.

The first such secondary hub has been in operation since mid-1991. The Southwest Kansas Library System, Dodge City, operates one of the seven regional library systems in the state. They service the interlibrary loan requests of their 15 KICNET member libraries in-system, and direct unfilled requests to KICPOST (the central hub) for redistribution to the rest of the network. This arrangement has worked well. The Southwest Kansas Library System is in the process of installing yet another cc:Mail feature, a fax gateway which will allow fax messages to be distributed via KICNET, and vice versa. If their experience with the cc:Mail fax gateway software proves successful, it may be implemented on a more widespread basis state-wide.

To accommodate short-term growth of the network, the Kansas State Library has recently acquired a second copy of the gateway (calling) software and a second 9,600bps modem. By using DESQview, the popular multitasking software, we can now call out to two libraries simultaneously with a single file server personal computer. This effectively almost doubles our capacity to support network participants.

The Kansas City Metropolitan Library Network (KCMLN), which spans the states of Kansas and Missouri, has recently installed cc:Mail software as a result of the successful state-wide network, KICNET. When the Missouri State Library can make the necessary arrangements for copies of the Missouri Union Catalog to be provided to Kansas libraries, a catalog exchange will take place, and the two cc:Mail-based interlibrary loan networks will be electronically linked, thus extending KICNET across state boundary lines.

Another exciting development is being spearheaded by the University of Kansas Law Library. They are considering the possibility of becoming a cc:Mail hub so that they can use e-mail to communicate with the heaviest-use legal firm clients of their library. In essence, they will create an e-mail reference querying and response system. Legal firms will pose reference questions to the Law Library electronically, and will receive their response in the same fashion (the response could potentially reference faxed or mailed information). A bridge would be established between the KU Law Library hub and the State Library hub, so that reference questions/ILL requests, after massaging by the Law Library staff, could be routed to other libraries in Kansas. The remote users of KU's network would dial into the Law Library hub.

Kansas enjoys the benefits of having the only graduate library school in the Plains region of the United States, the School of Library and Information Management, at Emporia State University. The library school became a KICNET participant in 1991, and is using the network to communicate class offering announcements state-wide, and to offer messaging and file transfer between students residing in remote KICNET communication sites state-wide and the library school campus. Many library school students are off-campus, practicing paraprofessionals in libraries throughout the state, and it is of value to them to be able to communicate with faculty and other students via electronic mail.

One major goal of the network is to provide a link to the Internet. This link to Internet is technically feasible, and simply awaits additional, modest funding. By installing cc:Mail to SMTP (Simple Mail Transfer Protocol) gateway on a personal computer server linked to a university's mainframe via a campus-wide Ethernet network, we could transform KICNET from a closed, private network to a linked network of the grandest proportions. cc:Mail users would address mail to Internet mailboxes using simple cc:Mail directory entries. cc:Mail itself would provide the proper links to Internet addresses. Because Simple Mail Transfer Protocol is the standard mail protocol for TCP/IP networks, compatibility with a wide variety of electronic mail systems is ensured. cc:Mail Link to SMTP runs on a designated gateway personal computer and works as a TCP/IP node connected to an Ethernet network. The link includes all TCP/IP and FTP software required on the personal computer side. cc:Mail Link to SMTP manages connections between its local cc:Mail post office and remote cc:Mail post offices, users of cc:Mail Remote, and foreign mail services in a manner transparent to the end user. The link translates outbound cc:Mail messages from the cc:Mail format to the format used by the SMTP protocol, namely RFC-822. In return, the link translates inbound SMTP messages into a format recognizable by cc:Mail.

cc:Mail Link to SMTP supports cc:Mail's ability to transfer binary and text files and facsimile items as mail attachments. Sending a program or fax item to colleagues over the SMTP mail network is simple and transparent. Incoming files are automatically inserted into a cc:Mail message as file items with no intervention required on the part of the cc:Mail user. Outgoing attachments are automatically encoded in the appropriate format and inserted into the body of the message.

Individual SMTP user names may be entered into the cc:Mail directory, or a remote post office entry may be established in the cc:Mail post office. cc:Mail users may then address messages in one of two ways. First, by simply selecting the SMTP user's name from the directory listing using cc:Mail's usual "point-and-shoot" method. Alternatively, users may select the SMTP post office name and, at the prompt, type any standard Internet user's complete name and address. Conversely, SMTP mail users address messages to cc:Mail users exactly as if they were using their native mail system. The address would include the cc:Mail user's SMTP name, plus the full domain name of the SMTP link gateway. The SMTP link is like any other SMTP node on a TCP/IP network. The administrative functions of the SMTP link enable foreign addresses to be hidden from cc:Mail users. cc:Mail users address mail to those using SMTP-based mail systems without the knowledge that they are not cc:Mail users. The cc:Mail SMTP Mail Directory provides this addressing transparency by automatically translating addresses from an eight-character SMTP name to their full 30-character cc:Mail name. Through an aliasing function, this same Mail Directory also routes mail from SMTP through cc:Mail to a user on another mail system. An Internet user could, for example, send to both a librarian using cc:Mail and an engineering student using UNIX Mail by sending only one message through a cc:Mail hub.

cc:Mail offers a number of WAN routing connections. Some of the technologies that cc:Mail supports include: repeaters (such as 3Com and DEC), bridges (such as Retix and Vitalink), routers (such as NetWare Link products, Cisco, and Wellfleet), asychronous modems (such as Hays and Telebit, speeds up to 38.4kbps, MNP error correction supported), modem pools (based on "Int 14," "NETCI" or "Int 6B"), callback modems (such as Universal Data Systems Model 224CG), null modem connections, dial-up and leased lines, land-based and satellite lines (the delays in satellite links cause no problems for cc:Mail), X.25 cards (Eicon), and X.25 networks or PBXs that use either 8- or 7-bit mode (very few personal computer products can support the common 7-bit mode).

KICNET, running cc:Mail, has proven to be an economical, rapid, reliable, and extremely popular system for the transmission of interlibrary loan messages. Participants responded to a request for evaluation of the network with universal praise.

Network Reliability

Perhaps the best thing about KICNET is that its e-mail software has never once, in the over two years of operation for our libraries, lost or garbled even one message. Software companies parade the word "bulletproof" all too frequently to describe the reliability of their programs. But, given cc:Mail's track record for Kansas libraries, and the literally hundreds of thousands of messages KICNET has carried, this software is one that truly deserves that praiseworthy appellation.

One extreme example of where any reasonable person might have expected cc:Mail to have dropped a few messages is one that I use advisedly. It has proven impossible for Kansas to shake the Wizard of Oz stereotype, and even though statistically, other states have more tornadoes than does Kansas, we do get our share. And one summer day in 1990, a massive tornado ripped through the small community of Hesston.

Both the public library and a private academic college in Hesston are KICNET participants. A KICNET communications session with Hesston College was, by sheer coincidence, in mid-session at the time the twister began its devastation. It is hard to transmit data between two modems when the telephone connection linking them is interrupted by downed telephone lines. The call was "abnormally interrupted," but when we called them back several days later when all telephone service was restored, cc:Mail picked up where it left off. Not even the record that was being transmitted when the phone line went dead was lost. We now brag that KICNET is "Kansas tornado-proof."

References and Notes

1. Like many states, Kansas has a core group of very large academic and public libraries, and literally hundreds of smaller public libraries and dozens of smaller academic libraries. This stratification of library resources resulted in a two-tiered OCLC "haves" and non-OCLC "have-nots."

2. Flanders, Bruce. 1989. *National Survey of Interlibrary Loan Networks.* Kansas State Library.

3. Flanders, Bruce. 1989. *Evaluation of ILL Alternatives. Kansas State Library.*

A Wide-Area Network Linking the Campuses of Arizona State University: A Library Perspective

Henry Harken, Electronic Information Specialist
Fletcher Library, Arizona State University West

Abstract

With the necessary expansion of Arizona State University from one to two campuses, ASU telecommunications staff went to work to link the two geographically distant sites. Telecommunications needs were integrated into the planning for the new campus; in fact, the utility tunnel through which telecom lines would run was constructed before any buildings on the new campus were erected. The resulting wide-area network connecting the two campuses, linked by fiber optics, dedicated twisted-pair telephone lines and microwave, was designed to allow for maximum flexibility in user access to the wide variety of computer resources on campus. The library OPAC is accessible via the telecom network, and is heavily used by dial-in access clients. Librarians have benefitted by access to modem pools and other telecommunications resources.

Rapid Growth Created Need for New Campus

The formation of ASU West was prompted by rapid growth. Arizona is still one of the most rapidly increasing population centers in the United States. Arizona State University (ASU) is located in Tempe, the municipality directly adjacent to the east side of Phoenix, and has long provided higher education to the valley. Originating as an ordinary school in the late nineteenth century, it became Arizona State College, then a university after the Second World War. Into the 1970s, the preponderance of the population settled in the east side of the valley, while the housing developments and industry began to grow to the west. In 1984, the Arizona legislature created a second campus of ASU to address the need for higher education in the west valley. One of the concerns during the creation of the campus was avoiding the duplication of existing University resources. This was recognized as being especially advantageous in the areas of mainframe computing and library automated catalog support. These resources are expensive to purchase and maintain, and, to take advantage of economy of scale, these resources needed to be linked when the new campus was constructed.

The campus sites are over seventeen miles apart but, the actual distance by road is greater than twenty-five miles, spanning congested city streets and highways. Providing effective voice, data, and video links over this distance was complicated and it was costly. ASU's Telecommunications Services (TCS) became the de facto provider and planning agency in fulfilling this need. TCS was expected by many parties to take this role with no additional funds for personnel or equipment on the Tempe side of the connection, and for support on the West campus.

Planning for the WAN

The true foundation for ASU's wide-area network was an RFP process begun by ASU Telecommunications Services in 1983, resulting in the installation of a broadband cable and software communications system on the Tempe campus. This project, called the Advanced Communication Support System (ACSS), provided an infrastructure for current and expected growth in communications including data, voice, and video. In 1985, installation began on a cabling plant consisting of three broadband cables, one fiber-optic cable, and twisted-pair cabling. On the Tempe campus alone, 335 miles of cable were installed. One broadband cable is used for voice and data, one has been set aside for video, and the third is a spare. Installing the cables together as part of the project meant less cost compared to installing each cable separately. The fiber-optic cable, though currently "unlit," provides the possibility of expansion into the higher speeds of the FDDI protocol when network densities make it desirable.

Telecommunications Expansion Costs

An investment in facilities of this magnitude includes associated costs. The cable plant alone cost over $4,000,000. Some representative costs follow:

Tempe campus cable plant	4,000,000
AT&T System 85 PBX	4,000,000
System 85 upgrade (4/90)	220,000
Ethernet channel on broadband	60,000
Ethernet presence in university buildings	1,120,000
Ongoing support of voice	50,000 to 200,000 per year
Ongoing growth in cable plant	50,000 to 150,000 per year

The considerable investment in TCS staff planning and support of this large network is difficult to quantify.

The active broadband system is composed of Hughes Lan Systems (formerly Sytek) hardware and software and allows great flexibility and utility for users and network administrators. A broadband system allows multiple independent networks to coexist on a single cable. A single broadband is more expensive and complicated than a baseband system (single carrier/network), but permits the installation of less cable. This technology does this by assigning a different frequency to each network, protocol, or purpose.

Wide Range of Data Services

The broadband hardware and software carries a wide range of data services. Two that have had the widest impact is an ASCII communications system (HLS System 2000), and an Ethernet channel. The ASCII communications system allows any user with a terminal, or personal computer, with a standard serial connection and communications software to communicate with a variety of hosts and network services. Even communications services that normally require special hardware or software, as in IBM 3270 type connections, for example, were available to users due to the connection of protocol converters between the host computer and the network. The connection of the campus Tandem computer made the catalog, with the offerings of the ASU libraries and other databases, searchable from offices or computing labs.

Soon after that, a dial-in modem pool, operating up to 2,400bps was established. It was now possible for faculty, students, and staff to connect to most services, allowing them to search library catalogs and databases, conduct electronic mail, or nearly any other service that was possible to do on-campus, from an off-campus site. ASU Telecommunications Service has since upgraded that service to include modems that operate under the international V.32 and V.42 standards, making available speeds up to 19.2mbps for access from off-campus.

Substantially lower hardware costs were an added benefit to users of the broadband connections. The average cost of installing a connection to the ASCII channel of the broadband was found to be approximately $500 plus the cost of a serial port, compared to an average $750 for an IBM 3270 terminal connection, and an additional $750 for an Irma 3270 board to be installed in the personal computer. A savings of over $1,000 per connection added up to a considerable savings on a campus of over 4,000 employees. Perhaps even more important was the flexibility and the range of computing services now available via this new communications connection. Users no longer needed a dedicated connection for each computer but could now communicate with a variety of computers through the one serial port.

Compliance with Major Telecommunications Protocols

The Ethernet channel on the broadband-based network has had a great impact on the computer and network users of ASU and will continue to expand in importance. Recognizing the emergence of international standards for communications between differing computing machinery, ASU Telecommunications Services and the computing and communications policy-making bodies recommended in 1989 that Ethernet and TCP/IP be the primary supported standards at ASU in this area. Products supporting TCP/IP were available for most of the computing machinery at ASU. An eventual migration to OSI was acknowledged as the likely next step in the latter half of the decade.

Telecommunications Support First Priority

In the early days of ASU West, the nucleus of faculty, administrators, and staff were housed and taught at temporary sites in the west valley. The West campus library began with a minuscule collection at one of these temporary locations. In 1985, planning began for a permanent home for the library, the first building to be built on the site purchased by the State in northwest Phoenix. ASU Telecommunications Services championed an important part of the campus infrastructure which was put in before ground was broken for a single building: a massive utility tunnel with the internal dimensions of ten feet square. The importance of putting this tunnel in before the campus was developed was based on experience at the Tempe campus where planners from just forty years ago could not have anticipated campus growth, especially the explosive increase in telecommunications needs and capabilities. Adding a utility tunnel later would have been an extremely expensive proposition. The tunnel at the West campus defined the internal perimeter of the planned first phase of the campus and provided the basis for intracampus telecommunications along with other critical services that are usually taken for granted.

Expanding Beyond T1

The ACSS broadband communications system was the foundation for the WAN connecting the ASU Tempe and ASU West campuses. The extension of the system to the West campus in the spring of 1988 was first made using a telephone company T1 cable. T1 lines operate at 1.544mbps, which is considerably slower than the broadband networking capacity at the Tempe campus, but for the early and relatively few occupants of the new campus, this was adequate. The T1 line carried several channels; to spread the load, part of the data load was also carried by dedicated telephone lines relocated from the temporary sites. The online catalog connections from Tempe to the West campus were initially handled through these dedicated lines.

As more faculty, administrators, and staff occupied the campus, the T1 became less viable as a sole solution for data communications between the campuses. A microwave link was planned, anticipating the growth and eventual need for even greater capacity. The microwave link between the two campuses became operational in 1991. It provides a two-way 45mbps video connection and sixteen T-1 links supporting voice and data communications between the two campuses. The landline T-1 is still being used during the shakedown period. It is anticipated that it will be retained as a permanent backup to the microwave connection.

One of the problems associated with microwave installations is the need for line-of-sight between transmitters and receivers. Though not really known as a mountainous area, the valley in which Phoenix resides includes buttes, and other large hills that make line-of-sight transmission difficult between Tempe and northwest Phoenix. Another problem was the continuing growth leading to larger buildings being constructed in the central corridor of the valley. The towers at both locations, large enough to surmount such obstacles, would have been aesthetically displeasing, not to mention cost prohibitive. The solution was to take advantage of another natural feature, South Mountain, that sits to the south of Phoenix. Long a location for transmission antennas, using a relay site on the mountain would increase the transmission distance but avoid the problem associated with line-of-sight.

Library Benefits

The ASU WAN has provided numerous benefits to the staff and library users of the Fletcher Library at ASU West. Upon moving into the new building, library reference staff with the ASCII channel connection were immediately able to access the many services on that network. The Fletcher Library staff relies heavily on the use of mainframe e-mail to better manage their time through messaging and calendaring. Previously, staff needed to use either dedicated 3270 terminals or microcomputers with 3270 boards installed. These 3270 connections used dedicated coaxial connections and provided access to the IBM mainframe, but not to any other service. With the ASCII channel solution on the broadband, the staff now had a wide range of options for computing because of the multitude of services now connected to the channel.

A major innovation was a newly available dial-out modem pool that became available in the spring of 1988. Each reference librarian had his own microcomputer to do word processing and online searching. Each formerly needed his own modem and analog telephone line to make the best use of his time. With the connection of the dial-out modem pool, any librarian with a connection to the ASCII channel had access to a modem. The end result was better management of library funds and resources.

The following year, the shared library system was made available on the ASCII channel, due to a change in software and added hardware. Library staff members, and for that matter, any ASU faculty or staff member with an ASCII connection now had access to the online catalog from their offices or service points. OPAC access was no longer restricted to the dedicated terminals located in the ASU libraries.

The advent of a dial-in modem pool with local telephone numbers on both sides of the valley created a library resource that was truly state-wide. Citizens of Arizona were given access to the state's largest online library catalog through this route. Before long, observers of computing and telecommunications in the state began seeing the library catalog listed on electronic bulletin boards, and use of the online catalog virtually exploded. It was not uncommon for information service staff at any of the ASU libraries to be approached by library users clutching printouts resulting from diligent searching of the online catalog from home computers.

The trend toward the use of Ethernet for networking has opened up another world of information resources to the library, and also faculty, staff, and students in offices and computing labs. Within the ASU West library, the local-area network used by all library staff was connected to the University Ethernet backbone using a Cayman Gatorbox gateway. The first function of this gateway was to provide TCP/IP services to the library staff. Access to the ASCII channel on the broadband is no longer needed for communications to any standard University computing resource. Communications speeds have been greatly increased from a typical 9,600bps to approximately 435kbps. Many other resources have also been made available within and outside the University through the Internet. Outside the Library, West campus student computing labs and faculty office network connections offer the full range of TCP/IP services and access to Internet resources via the WAN connections between campuses. Early library planning anticipated making dedicated library terminals available throughout the campus, but the Ethernet connections have made this plan superfluous: the Tandem computer on which the online catalog resides has an Ethernet port and access has become universally available at ASU West.

The ASU Ethernet backbone on the WAN has provided external communications to many of the University's LANs; the ASU TCS policy on protocols is quite permissive. The backbone carries a variety of networking protocols besides TCP/IP, including DECNet, Banyan, Appletalk, and IPX. The LAN at the ASU West Library runs Appletalk over Localtalk and Ethernet, and may communicate with a large number of similar Appletalk zones residing on both campuses.

LAN-based electronic mail may be the next major WAN service to be implemented as ASU moves further into a distributed computing environment. The X.400 standard is being considered in the planning process, and X.500 is anticipated. The ASU West Library and other users of the WAN will benefit as existing and new software integrates communications with other applications.

Victim of Its Own Success

Ultimately, the existing hardware and software of the wide-area network will become a victim of its own success. They will be outgrown when, in the future, the many applications using communications links (especially imaging) will tax the current bandwidth beyond its capacity. But, with the two spare broadbands and an unlit fiber-optic cable as currently untapped physical resources, ASU should be able to accommodate communciations standards that will provide speeds in excess of 1GBps. Library applications will be able to take advantage of this bandwidth by offering new imaging applications, high-speed document delivery, and services that have not yet been conceived.

The Ohio Library and Information Network (OhioLINK)

Len Simutis, Ph.D., Executive Director
The Ohio Library and Information Network

Abstract

OhioLINK will link major universities and college libraries in Ohio to provide access to printed and electronic materials. Planned and managed by the Ohio Board of Regents, OhioLINK is based on Digital Equipment Corporation DECsystem 5500 RISC/ULTRIX systems as a common platform, running Innovative Interface library automation software. This chapter describes OhioLINK network planning and administration, as well as the use of the high-speed OARnet TCP/IP network for telecommunications links.

The OhioLINK Project: An Overview

The Ohio Library and Information Network (OhioLINK) is designed to provide shared state-wide access to the materials available in the state's university and college libraries, and the State Library of Ohio. It will also provide access to the materials stored in electronic format through a linkage of computer systems interconnected via a state telecommunications system, and will serve as a gateway to the extensive information resources now available on computer networks nationally and internationally.

OhioLINK will connect university libraries throughout the state so that they will appear to the user as a single resource of over 20 million volumes. Faculty and students who wish to borrow materials from other OhioLINK libraries will know the circulation status of each item, and will be able to request delivery of available materials in print form to the person's home campus within 48 hours; if the information is available in electronic format, delivery will be in a matter of minutes.

OhioLINK is supporting development of advanced workstation hardware and software to provide sophisticated search and retrieval capabilities for electronic document access and display. As more information becomes available in electronic format for full text and graphics, the limits of terminal-based library automation systems will need to be augmented by more powerful and accessible computer workstations. Development of the workstation hardware and software is a critical element in the extension of

OhioLINK into the emerging fields of electronic publishing, imaging, and collaborative faculty-student research and teaching now made possible by advanced telecommunications networks.

Initially, OhioLINK will be available at 15 public and two private universities and at the State Library of Ohio, but the system is expected to be extended to the two-year college system as soon as practicable. Longer term, OhioLINK will provide the mechanism for resource-sharing among Ohio's public and private colleges and universities, and with large municipal libraries with extensive and valuable research holdings. OhioLINK is also expected to build upon private sector initiatives in the new "information industry" evident in the services provided by Chemical Abstracts, CompuServe, Mead Data (Lexis and Nexis), Predicasts, and OCLC, all based in Ohio.

Implementation of the OhioLINK system began in July 1991 with the establishment of a central site for a union catalog and journal citation databases at Wright State University, and the installation of compatible hardware and software on six campuses during 1991-92. The remaining eleven universities and the State Library of Ohio will implement the system in 1992-94. The expansion of journal citation and full-text databases is expected to play an important role in implementing the system, as is electronic delivery of documents, either via information brokers, or via direct storage of the materials on OhioLINK systems.

The computer hardware systems being installed are Digital Equipment Corporation (DEC) minicomputer systems running the UNIX operating system, and using TCP/IP protocols for inter-system communications. Just as the organizational aspects of the OhioLINK project needed to take into account the changing nature of social participation in the development of operating policy and procedures, so the system will take advantage of changes in the computing environment which emphasize decentralization and cooperative computing via networking.

The Origins of OhioLINK

The OhioLINK project is a cooperative venture of the state's university libraries and the Ohio Board of Regents, which has overall responsibility for the conduct of higher education in the state. Like OCLC (which began with funding from the Board of Regents as the Ohio College Library Center in the 1960s), OhioLINK has its origins in a consortial arrangement of universities and the Board of Regents with a common purpose of improving access to information to support instruction and research.

OhioLINK grew out of the work done by the Ohio Board of Regents' Library Study Committee which was appointed in 1986 to make recommendations on how the state could respond to the rising number of requests for new university library facilities. Although the committee's principal focus was on facilities and library storage, their research paved the way for the examination of options that might improve the quality of academic library services and operations. In addition to a recommendation for the adoption of regional remote storage facilities (four of which are under construction or in advanced stages of planning), the committee recommended that "the State of Ohio implement as expeditiously as possible a state-wide electronic catalog system."

In response, The Board of Regents established a Steering Committee representing librarians, faculty, academic administrators, and computer systems managers from campuses throughout Ohio. The Steering Committee created three task forces: one on the user's view; one representing the librarians' view; and the third representing the computer systems and networking view. Through meetings, public hearings, and conferences, the Steering Committee subsequently prepared an RFI (February 1989), and an RFP (August 1989), for the library systems component of the project. A contract with Innovative Interfaces, Inc., of Berkeley, California, was established for development and delivery of software, and the installation of Digital Equipment Corporation hardware began in July 1991. Separate but related RFPs and contracts will be prepared for the experimental workstation and citation and full-text database components of the project for implementation in 1992.

Organizational and Administrative Issues

Higher education in Ohio has a strong tradition of institutional autonomy. Funding for each university is distributed by the Board of Regents on a formula basis indexed to level and size of enrollment and degree program mix. There is no line item budgeting, and each institution is free to distribute the "state subsidy" as it is called, as it wishes. Each university is also free to set their own tuition and fee rates, although recently, the legislature has set tuition "caps" in an effort to control increasing costs for students and their parents.

OhioLINK, as a creation of the Board of Regents, needed to develop an organizational model which fit the decentralized structure of its other programs. The decentralization pattern affects not only the organization and staffing for OhioLINK, but also the computer and networking architecture that was adopted for the project.

From the start, the system was designed to assure universities that the policies they had been using regarding lending practices, materials acquisitions, and internal library organization patterns would be respected in implementing the system. As might be expected, the organizational frameworks for libraries varies considerably; some have unified collections for the various academic and professional schools; others have separate collections and distinct organizations to deal with medical and law schools.

In the development of the project, OhioLINK worked with the directors of the academic libraries only, and these directors were expected to work with directors of professional libraries on their campuses. As a consequence, some of the law and medical collections will be part of the initial OhioLINK system, and others will not be until these separate professional school libraries choose to migrate to a common library automation environment and commit to participating in the sharing of physical and electronic documents in the consortium. Both the law and medical libraries are already a part of state or regional consortia for other purposes, so there is a framework of cooperation already in place which OhioLINK may be able to take advantage of over time.

In the conduct of the RFP process for selecting the library automation system, a large number of "library function" committees were formed to draft RFP specifications, develop evaluation criteria, and participate in vendor demonstrations and site visits that led to the selected vendor. Committee membership was drawn in most instances from professional library staff at each institution, but in order to make committee size manageable, most committees had eight or fewer members. When greater institutional involvement was required, the committees would conduct hearings or open meetings to expand the participation in discussion around particular topics. The original committees were created to address catalog creation and maintenance; OPAC; Circulation and Interlibrary Loan; Document Delivery; Acquisitions and Serials; and Collection Management and Development. The work of these committees was coordinated by the OhioLINK director of library systems—who also had the lead responsibility for creating the RFP document and establishing a vendor evaluation framework.

In the implementation phase of OhioLINK, which is now well underway, these functional committees have been reconstituted, with some membership changes, but with a strong effort to control committee size once again to a manageable number. Additional committees are being formed for work on database preparation, retrospective conversion, the workstation project, and journal/full-text databases, with additional members being drawn from the faculty and from computing systems as appropriate.

As an integral part of the implementation process, representatives from each of the six universities installing systems during 1991-92 are meeting as an implementation task force. It is the responsibility of the task force to identify policy issues that will need to be addressed and resolved by the appropriate functional committees, to share implementation plans and procedures for each campus with colleagues, and to work with OhioLINK administration in coordinating implementation with the library automation vendor, the computer equipment manufacturers, the state-wide telecommunications network, and campus networking and computing personnel. The participants in meetings of the task force will vary from meeting to meeting based on the topics under discussion, but continuity is maintained through participation by the "lead implementor" on each campus as designated by the director of libraries.

Once the vital issues are identified and formulated as policy recommendations, they are taken up in turn by the Library Advisory Council, and if appropriate, by the Policy Advisory Council. The Library Advisory Council is composed of the directors of libraries at the seventeen OhioLINK institutions, and a representative from the two-year college. The Council is chaired by a member selected by vote of the Council. The OhioLINK executive director, the director of the State Library of Ohio, and a representative from the law libraries serve ex officio. (Two of the OhioLINK institutions are medical schools, thus the medical libraries have direct participation.)

The OhioLINK Policy Advisory Council is comprised of eighteen voting members; seventeen members from each of the OhioLINK institutions, and a two-year college representative. Membership includes at least three faculty members, four library directors, three computer center directors, three academic deans, and two system librarians. The OhioLINK executive director and the director of OARnet (the state-wide academic telecommunications network) serve ex officio. The chair of the Policy Advisory Council is selected from among the voting members.

The Library Advisory Council and the Policy Advisory Council report through the executive director to the OhioLINK Governing Board, which is comprised of nine university provosts selected from OhioLINK institutions, and a two-year college representative. The chancellor of the Ohio Board of Regents, the OhioLINK executive director, and the chairs of the Policy and Library Advisory Councils serve ex officio (see Figure 1). The Chair of the Governing Board is selected from among its members by vote each year. In creating the Governing Board, the Board of Regents believed that the direct involvement of the senior academic officers from participating OhioLINK institutions would assure that the system will address the broad academic and research needs of faculty and students.

Each of these three groups meet regularly, and with the establishment of committees and task forces in more specific areas, the logistics of scheduling, meeting, and sharing information among the groups and the larger community is quite formidable. In the early stages, this difficulty was compounded since no permanent staff beyond the executive director position was employed on the project until July 1991—and then, only modestly, relative to the overall scale of the project. This has meant a continued reliance on the good will and cooperation provided by the significant voluntary effort by library administrators and staff, computing and networking administrators and

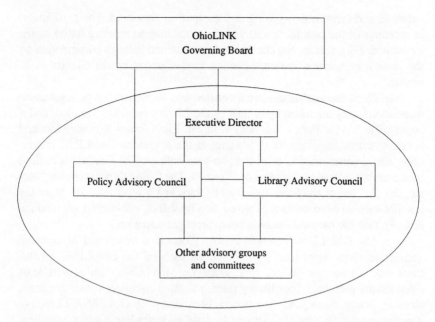

Figure 1. OhioLINK governance.

staff, and academic administrators and faculty. The degree of participation to date—in fact, the very success of the project—is due in large part to the shared recognition of the long-term value of the project and the common interests of the library, computing, and academic research communities in developing an exemplary state-wide program.

Technological Issues

The OhioLINK model for computer systems and networking was driven not by technological imperatives and opportunities, but by the traditions of decentralization and institutional autonomy that characterize public higher education in Ohio. The Steering Committee, in fact, had originally hoped that the computer system architecture could be built around the linkage of disparate systems, with common protocols and standards for data access and data storage as the basis for shared system development. However, neither the adoption of consistent standards, nor the cooperation among library automation system vendors had proceeded sufficiently to allow for this approach to be used in building OhioLINK initially.

Still, there was good reason not to opt for a system which was highly centralized with access via dedicated terminals, for this conjured up the creation of one monolithic computer system run by the state, rather than a collaborative undertaking by participating institutions. So the Steering Committee concluded that even though the ability for disparate systems to communicate with one another was not yet in the marketplace, it would be important to build the system in such a way that the computer architecture incorporated a considerable amount of discretion and independence for each campus, while providing an overall framework which allowed for compatibility among systems.

A second major consideration in the design of the computer systems was to take advantage of existing state investments in computer networking rather than build a separate, dedicated communications network to support OhioLINK. The state-wide telecommunications network, OARnet, (the Ohio Academic Resources Network), had been created initially to provide access to the Ohio Supercomputer Center in Columbus (see Figure 2). Since supercomputer use is not only computationally intensive, but increasingly focused on graphic representation of results, the bandwidth provided by OARnet was considerable, with the capacity to grow rather dramatically to meet computationally intensive requirements. The decision was made early on to take advantage of the existing investment in networking, and to expand OARnet as required to meet OhioLINK telecommunications requirements.

OARnet delivers T1 (1.5 megabit) services to nearly every Ohio-LINK campus today, and there is provision to provide fractional T3 (45 megabit) service as needed during the next two years. This additional bandwidth will be of particular importance as OhioLINK moves to electronic document delivery, although it is not currently judged to be required for day-to-day operations of document check-out and delivery.

A third technological factor for the OhioLINK project is the recognition that systems built around terminal connections will be found unsatisfactory as faculty and students continue to increase the power of computing available to them on the desktop. They do not have the level of computer functionality that people have come to expect through the use of personal computers, and they fall far short of the capabilities of more advanced personal computer systems and workstations. Rather than continue the use of low-end terminal-based systems, OhioLINK committed to the delivery of its major functional capabilities through high-end workstations.

The workstation, rather than the main library automation system, will be the focus for the development of experimental software for the display and analysis of information resources. As the price of desktop computing continues to decline, it makes sense to invest in development of access and analysis tools that will be based on these sophisticated personal computer systems. The other reason to focus on workstations rather than terminal connections is that advances in networking are fully available to those running

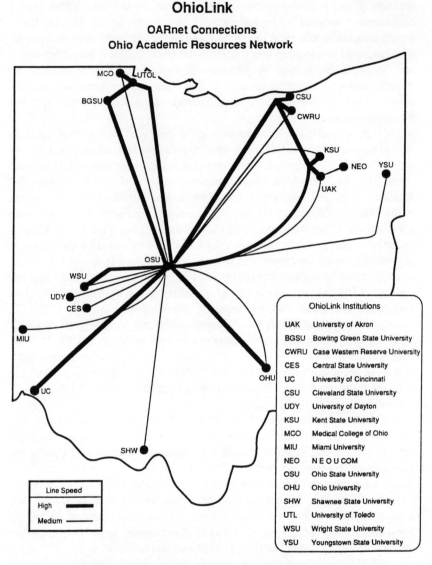

Figure 2. The Ohio Academic Resource Network (OARnet).

workstations, and that over time, the principal computing environment for faculty will be workstations rather than terminal connections to mainframes.

The same approach should also be applied to access to the Ohio-LINK system by library staff. Much of the functionality required for sophisticated cataloging, record editing, and connection to remote databases, simply cannot be provided for library staff via terminal emulation. A significant investment, then, needs to be made in high-end computer workstations which will facilitate the work of library staff, facilitate their interaction with faculty and students who will increasingly have advanced workstations for their daily work, and to assure that library professionals are not disenfranchised technologically in the conduct of their work.

OhioLINK will also provide state-wide access to journal citation databases, and full-text databases as they become available. Access to these central databases will be via the Internet using TCP/IP protocols, and from the campus OhioLINK systems. There are expected to be economies of scale associated with making journal citation databases available to a large number of participating institutions. OhioLINK may well provide access to non-commercial sources of information, such as research proposals and grants received by OhioLINK universities, copies of reports prepared for or by the Ohio Board of Regents, and descriptions of special collections or other unique resources that may be of interest to faculty and students.

One other aspect of technology needs to be mentioned in describing the project. Reference was made earlier to the difficulties of communications brought on by the large number of participants and the need for frequent meetings. As a response to some of these communications concerns, a computer-based electronic bulletin board was established as a forum for discussion of implementation issues, and as a vehicle for communication of agendas, minutes, and other formal summaries of OhioLINK activities. To date, over 175 people have subscribed to the discussion group, and it has proven to be a lively forum for discussion of a variety of issues related to project implementation. As campuses begin installation of hardware and software, it is anticipated that the electronic discussion group will have both operational and archival value to project participants.

OhioLINK—The User's Perspective

The OhioLINK system was built from the perspective of the need for students and faculty to have better information access tools as well as better physical access to the holdings of Ohio's university libraries. Thus, the creation of a central catalog grew out of the need to display circulation status for items, not from the intent of creating a union catalog, or enhanced cataloging capabilities. Students and faculty wish to know not only if an item has been catalogued, but if it is available to be circulated. They also wish to have a more rapid delivery system than that provided by interlibrary loan, and they also wish to be able to initiate checkout and delivery of materials not only from the library, but from a dorm room, faculty office, or departmental computer lab. Similarly, the delivery of copies of articles in facsimile or image format should be possible to printers distributed across the campus, and not just to an office in the library. These functional requirements, then, dictated a more accessible system, with considerable user-initiated actions, and with a system that depended heavily on a high bandwidth network to keep track of circulation status, support patron-initiated checkout, manage document delivery, allow for place-independent access to OhioLINK databases across the network, and the delivery of materials to a large number of highly decentralized locations in physical and electronic formats.

The system is designed to allow faculty and students to search their campus systems initially for bibliographic items of interest. If the items are unavailable or none are found, the search is passed to the OhioLINK central site. If items of interest are found and available, the system will then allow the patron to request delivery of the items by having the patron authenticated to the system, and then a circulation transaction is initiated by the patron. The system then routes the request to the appropriate library as a circulation request, appropriate routing indicators are printed, and the materials are delivered to the borrower's campus. To support the display of circulation status, as each item is checked out or in at a participating library, a transaction code is transmitted to the central site to update information on circulation status.

A similar focus on the user's perspective is evident in access to journal citation databases. These databases will be located at the central site and will be accessible either as a menu pick from the campus OPAC, or by direct connection via TCP/IP protocols. When searches are made against the databases, the retrieved items are matched with the library's serials holdings files, so that the availability of a particular journal is known to the user. In the near future, it is expected that journal citation databases will be linked to image databases which store the contents of journal articles. The patron will then be able to request delivery of a copy of the article across the network, or if connected to the system with an appropriate workstation and display, download the article to the workstation.

Beyond WANs: OhioLINK as a Value-Added Network (VAN)

The benefits to faculty and students which have been the design impetus for OhioLINK are expected to provide a major improvement in locating and accessing appropriate information to support teaching, scholarship, and research. While to date there has not been an emphasis on the development of tools that explicitly benefit individual library professionals, OhioLINK will make available a number of analytical and access tools for librarians which will provide major collective benefits to library operations. For example, wide-area network access to the central site bibliographic database, when combined with reports and analyses of circulation, can provide valuable information for collection management and development. Long-term, there could be profound changes in individual library acquisitions policies as the document delivery system is implemented, and as libraries become more aware, in real time, of the collective results of individual collection development decisions. There certainly will be economies of scale associated with acquiring and maintaining journal citation databases, and network access to these databases may obviate, over time, the need for some CD-ROMs on local-area networks, and the expense associated with managing them at individual libraries. Patron-initiated checkout and document delivery also should, in the longer term, allow for redirection of staff activities that support interlibrary loan, and shift much of the time- and labor-intensive aspects of ILL to more productive purposes.

So the OhioLINK WAN will provide a number of opportunities for cost containment or cost avoidance through shared access to printed and electronic materials, and better information about acquisitions and circulation that can influence collection development. The intriguing potential of wide-area networks such as OhioLINK, however, is tied to the emergence of what can be called value-added networks (VANs). Value-added networks build on the economies of scale and shared access provided by WANs by adding layers of information which augment the original sources or transform their uses. For example, a bibliographic record might be retrieved from the OhioLINK central site, but in the process of transmitting the information to the user, pointers to or display of additional information could be provided. For example, a retrieved bibliographic record might identify a subject heading for U.S. Biography, which in turn would point to or transmit an entry in Who's Who. A table of contents database might be accessed and the contents transmitted when conference proceedings were retrieved. A photograph of the author might appear in the display of the bibliographic record, or illustrations contained in the book might be transmitted when the record is retrieved.

These value-added services will depend on a linking of disparate databases to retrieve and display supplementary information that takes advantage of distributed computing and high bandwidth. It moves away from the traditional unit-record approach to bibliographic records—i.e., all relevant information is encoded within the individual MARC record—to one which incorporates distributed, dynamic database linkages. Many of these distributed databases are likely to be provided by commercial information services, information brokers, or by traditional publishers. For example, a faculty member may be interested in purchasing a newly published book. She would search the OhioLINK database, find an ISBN number, then dynamically link to the inventory control databases for bookstores in her area. Using this capability, she could then order the book, or perhaps only order specific chapters after reviewing the table of contents and have the materials shipped to her local printer.

Over time, value-added service providers are likely to emerge which provide customized bibliographic retrieval services, online notification of new materials of interest by defined user search profiles, table of contents servers, illustration and animation servers, customized formatting and print servers, and dynamic annotation capabilities. Dynamic annotation is already finding its way into experimental electronic journals (when you retrieve an article you retrieve all subsequent references to the article as well). Some of these value-added services will also be of importance to the library professional with services such as real-time authority changes, computer programs which serve as agents to search serially through hundreds of OPACS to find specific items and confirm their availability for ILL, and just-in-time orders for reserve materials with appropriate copyright clearances.

The ultimate economic value of a new highway depends not only on connecting city A and city B, but also on the range of services and facilities that are provided along the highway. Sites adjacent to the highway benefit from the speed and ease of access, and eventually may provide services of even greater value than those at the end points—the now familiar shopping center vs. downtown department store phenomenon. The same process is likely to occur as new services and facilities are attached to the new information "highways" like OhioLINK and mechanisms to provide linkages and access are put in place. In this context, then, state-wide WAN projects like OhioLINK could prove to be a valuable test site for new and enhanced services provided by the professional library community and by the private sector, services which will ultimately improve the quality and effectiveness of scholarship and research.

JANET: The Educational and Research Network of the United Kingdom

Peter Stone, Information Services
University of Sussex Library, United Kingdom

Abstract

JANET, the United Kingdom Joint Academic Network, was established in 1984 by the Computer Board for Universities and Research Councils, and is now funded by its successor, the Information Systems Committee (ISC) of the Universities Funding Council. JANET links users to the facilities of over 2,000 registered computers on approximately 200 sites within the UK, using its own protocols to provide all the standard network services for collaboration and communication: electronic mail, interactive terminal-to-host access (remote login), file transfer, and remote job submission. Gateway services provide access to all the world's major public and research networks. However, as OSI begins to offer a wider range of facilities to reach computer users worldwide, OSI applications (for example, mail and directory services) are increasingly becoming available on JANET. Most recently, the structures needed to carry TCP/IP protocols, used on the world-wide Internet, are being put into place.

Almost all universities, polytechnics, and related institutions of higher education, as well as the institutes funded by the research councils, in England, Wales, Scotland, and Northern Ireland, are connected. This academic community comprises around 100,000 staff and 900,000 students. There is also a growing number of industrial and commercial organizations attached, all working in collaboration with members of the academic community. Of specific interest to libraries, the British Library, the National Libraries of Scotland and Wales, SLS, Blackwells, and OCLC, are all directly linked, and many more suppliers and utilities can be reached through gateways to other networks world-wide.

This study of the network and the use made of it is particularly intended for those working on the development of information services and of library operations on other networks.

Development 1984-1992

JANET was inaugurated on April 1, 1984, replacing a variety of networks set up over the previous ten years to support scientific research. The first British networks had been established as "star networks" based on nationally-funded facilities at London, Manchester, Edinburgh, and the Rutherford Appleton Laboratory near Oxford. Later, regional networks, MIDnet and SWUCnet for example, had been set up to link available resources. Many of these early networks were mutually incompatible. By 1983, however, over 3,000 research grant holders of the Science and Engineering Research Council had access to the main computing facilities over the major research network, SERCnet. The following year they were combined into JANET, and the UK had a single academic network linking all universities and the major research centers.

Figure 1. JANET, the Joint Academic NETwork: Trunk lines and Network Operation Centres.

Since that time, the number of sites connected to JANET has substantially increased. The major group of institutions to establish connections were the polytechnics and the Scottish Central Institutions: tertiary-level colleges providing degrees predominantly in technology and in professional and vocational studies. In 1984, the polytechnics were funded separately, with no central support for research computing, and few found the resources to fund an individual connection. In 1989, the Polytechnics and Colleges Funding Council was established, and by 1991 the recurrent costs of their connection to JANET were centrally funded. At the same time, many of the Colleges of Higher Education were also linked. Over the last six years, numerous individual (but often government funded) institutes have connected, motivated largely by their working research collaboration with the universities. Several major libraries not funded by the Department of Education and Science, like the British Library, the National Libraries of Scotland, and of Wales are now connected. Most recently, following a redefinition of the regulations, several industrial research units and commercial suppliers have joined.

In common with many of the world's research networks, JANET is currently seeking ways in which to extend access to a wider range of users. The present infrastructure is largely based on the assumption that institutions connected justify a full X.25 high-bandwidth link direct to a relatively well-developed campus-sized LAN. This is clearly inappropriate for tertiary-level colleges, isolated research laboratories, and independent libraries. A framework is under discussion in which such institutions willing to abide by agreed conditions of use can nonetheless have economic access to electronic mail, limited interactive connections for database searching, or contribute their own services.

The network is configured to provide high-speed multiple links between switches at the eight Network Operation Centres (NOCs) (see Figure 1). This ensures that if the line between any two of these sites is interrupted, then traffic can be re-routed elsewhere around the network. The NOCs are based in university computing centers or in major laboratories of the Science and Engineering Research Council (SERC). Each of the individual institutions (around 200) is itself linked by a single leased line to the nearest NOC. Following the major JANET Mk II upgrade almost all universities are now connected by a 2MB line; smaller sites may use a 64, 48, or even a 9.6kbps line (see Figure 2).

The infrastructure of JANET is in effect an internet formed from a large number of interconnected sub-networks, thus providing widespread connectivity both within the community and to external services and other communities. At the majority of sites, local-area networks based on CSMA/CD (Ethernet) and slotted ring technologies are connected to JANET through a gateway or a campus packet-switching exchange. It is estimated that several

Speed: the growth of UK academic networking

	To deliver a page (3000 characters)		
1970-85	**7 mins**	Telex	(75bps)
	(In practice 3.5 mins by using restricted character set)		
1974-87	**1.6 mins**	Modem	(300bps)
1984-90	**12.5 secs**	Asynchronous/PAD	(2400bps)
1985-89	**3.1 secs**	File transfer over JANET	(9600 bps)
1989-91.	**0.5 secs**	-- -- -- --	(64000 bps)
1991-95	**70 pages/sec**	-- -- -- --	(2mbps) (max)
1990-94?	**300 pages/sec**	Ethernet across campus	(10mbps) (max)
1995?-	**5000 pages/sec**	SuperJanet	(150mbps) (max)
		- and ASCII text is obsolete.	

Scope and distance: the growth of UK academic network (dates are approximate)

1970-	Libraries use modems over direct 'phone lines for long-distance database searching
1980-	SERCnet. FTP (and login) to and from supercomputers (e.g. Atlas Centre)
1984-	JANET. Login/mail/ftp across UK.
	Mail (but not login) to Arpanet & Bitnet in US.
1988-	Campus networks widespread. Internet established in US.
	University library online catalogues (OPACS) common.
1991-	IXI & "Guest Telnet" provide international login.
	CWISs and major text databases connect
1992-	OSI standards lead to a global Directory, universal email, uniform interfaces
1993-	SuperJANET delivers full document images to the requestor's desk.

Figure 2. Growth of UK academic networking, technical dimesions, 1984.

thousand host computers and workstations, using a mix of over 20 operating systems, serve a population of over 50,000 terminals and personal computers. There are over 1,750 electronic mail services, over 2,000 systems supporting file transfer, and over 350 supporting networked remote job transfer and management.

Protocols and Standards

JANET is an X.25 packet-switched network conforming to the international CCITT standards, in common with most European and commercial networks. Until recently, TCP/IP traffic, as used on the Internet, was all translated at the NSFNet-Relay gateway, but in the last quarter of 1991 the JANET IP service was inaugurated, routing TCP/IP packets within X.25 frames.

The Coloured Books and the Transition to OSI

JANET provides all the standard network services for collaboration and communication: electronic mail, interactive terminal-to-host access (remote login), file transfer, and remote job submission. The network is currently in the middle of a transition to Open Systems Interconnection (OSI) standards: X.400 for mail, etc. They will soon replace the Coloured Book Protocols, so-called because each specification is bound in a differently colored cover (Blue Book, for example, covers file transfer). According to Bob Cooper, current Director of Networking, these were "developed in the UK as an interim set of standards for open networking prior to the availability of suitable international standards." They comprise "a pragmatic mix of international, UK, and academic community-defined standards that together provide a coherent architecture capable of supporting a range of applications over an infrastructure of interconnected LANs and WANs of different technologies." Manufacturers produce the software to meet the requirements and it is then tested by the Joint Network Team (see below) for conformance.

The JANET IP Service

By 1990 there was a considerable number of users who wished to network applications using the TCP/IP protocols, originally devised by Robert Kahn and Vint Cerf in 1974 and developed by the U.S. Department of Defense for DARPAnet. Nowadays TCP/IP effectively defines the scope world-wide of the Internet, and comes bundled with most workstations: with UNIX it is the Esperanto of distributed processing. Its huge growth in popularity now appears to threaten the adoption world-wide of at least some of the second generation of OSI networking standards proposed by ISO—the International Standards Organization.

The demand for TCP/IP has been created by the large range of software and equipment available, by the need to get access to information and to collaborate in research world-wide, and by the wish to "interwork" specialized applications within the community. OSI products exist for many needs, and access to the U.S. Federal Internet is now reasonably easy (through the NSFNet-Relay, see below), but full participation in research across campus, across the United Kingdom, or internationally, will require multiprotocol working for both information users *and* information providers. The implications are not widely understood, but already some UK university libraries are installing TCP/IP ports to their OPAC alongside the X.25, and warning of the greater complexity of multiprotocol software and/or terminal services needed for PC networking on campus.

Equally, X-Windows applications have developed rapidly over the last few years in workstation environments, all based on TCP/IP networking: the JNT (Joint Network Team) is currently working closely with ANSI, EWOS (the European Workshop on Open Systems), and other parties worldwide to devise a solution using ISO standards.

The Coloured Book Protocols (mentioned above) adopted by the Joint Network Team from the late 1970s were an expedient mix of standards, always intended to be replaced, in due course, by internationally agreed standards. In 1987, The Transition to OSI was accepted as the working policy. However, by 1990 the popularity of TCP/IP had made such a single-minded strategy unworkable. In 1991 the Computer Board approved a proposal from the JNT to develop the JANET IP Service, JIPS, to be made available through the computer centers of linked institutions. JIPS will support applications not provided by Coloured Books or OSI where there is an important service requirement (for example, X-Windows and Distributed File systems), and applications where the IP-based service adds significant value (for example, file transfer using Arpa-ftp and Telnet). SMTP mail, and NFS, being difficult to scale, will be discouraged. The plan is to use IP "tunnelling" over X.25 in which IP packets are wrapped within the X.25 frames. There will be links to the U.S. Federal Internet via the "fat pipe," (transatlantic undersea line) and to European IP networks via IXI. IXI is an X.25-based network carrying X.29 interactive traffic and X.400 electronic mail.

In 1991 eight institutions ran a pilot project known enigmatically as "Shoestring" and in November 1991 an invitation was sent to all institutions to connect a router to the JANET line for participation.

Gateways and Linked Networks

JANET maintains several gateways to the other academic networks that now link most of Europe, North America, and much of the Pacific rim (for example, IXI, EARN/BITNET, NSFnet, the Internet, and USENET) and through PSS (Packet Switch System) to interactive, and X.400 mail, services on the public networks. The EAN gateway will close in March 1992. The network itself (within the scope of "acceptable use") is completely "open" to incoming calls, though most of the computers attached to it accept only approved users. However no registration is needed to use the many library catalogs, and most of the other information services. They can be therefore easily consulted by users of British Telecom's Packet SwitchStream (PSS) network, and the academic networks that support interactive working.

EARN and BITNET

All sites on JANET are effectively connected to BITNET, EARN, and their linked networks world-wide through a single gateway based at the Rutherford Appleton Laboratory with the address UKACRL for inward calls to JANET (and EARN-RELAY outward). This relay converts incoming and outgoing mail to and from the JANET "Grey Book standard" and the BSMTP standard used over the IBM RSCS protocols. The use of a single gateway accounts for the absence of UK entries in BITNET's address list, whereas many U.S. sites provide both Internet and BITNET addresses to the same machine. A direct link to the Internet may be a more economical arrangement, and in late 1991 JANET's continuing membership of the EARN Association, the European BITNET network, was in question.

The NSFNet-Relay and the Internet

Communication between JANET sites in the United Kingdom, and ARPAnet sites in the United States has been provided for many years through a relay service operated at the University of London. Initially open only to researchers on approved grants, the services have been progressively opened to all users: first mail, then FTP, then in 1991 interactive use. Data is transmitted through a single transatlantic undersea line—the so-called "fat pipe"—of sufficiently high capacity (512kbps) to support even video conferencing. It is important to understand that this is a *relay* service, to which users (from either side of the Atlantic) must login before making a further onward call using the other protocol (see Figure 3).

File transfers between JANET's "Blue Book" protocol, OSI FTAM and the Internet FTP are routed through the FT-RELAY Service. Contact liaison@ft-relay.ac.uk.

UKnet Gateway

The UUCP gateway between JANET and UKnet, the network of computers in the United Kingdom that use the UNIX-UNIX communications protocol, is maintained at the University of Kent at Canterbury (UKnet@ukc.ac.uk). UKnet is part of EUnet, the European network, which is attached to the world-wide USENET news service network. Use of this gateway is not free, but the ISC does fully fund the use of the gateway from ISC-funded computers based in university computer centers. Contact postmaster@uknet.ac.uk.

The NSFNET Relay at ULCC now supports a guest Internet-to-JANET
terminal access service. This converts the communication protocols used on
the Internet to those used on JANET. Accounts are no longer essential.

A full guide to this service can be retrieved by mailing
```
info-server@nsfnet-relay.ac.uk
```
with the following text in the message:
```
Request: janetpad
Topic: userguide
```

In summary:
1. telnet to `sun.nsfnet-relay.ac.uk` – currently 128.86.8.7
2. login as `janet` – in lowercase; there is no password
3. enter the NRS name of a JANET host when prompted.
   This MUST be in UK order, i.e. `uk.ac.janet.news`

If you have any comments on the service please send them by e-mail to:
```
janetpad@nsfnet-relay.ac.uk.
```

Any further enquiries should be sent by e-mail to:
```
liaison@nsfnet-relay.ac.uk.
```

Email to addresses on JANET from BITNET and the Internet.
The pattern of mail addresses used within JANET is different from that on
many research networks. They are easily converted: just turn the elements of
the node-name around, so that it ends "AC.UK" rather than starts "UK.AC".

For example, queries from a user on BITNET about JANET-OPACS should
be sent to:
LIBRARY@CLUSTER.SUSSEX.AC.UK

Figure 3. Access to JANET from the Internet.

The Link to IXI and European Member Networks of RARE

In May 1990 the IXI backbone network started operation, running from Amsterdam to Bern, and connecting the academic and research networks of 17
European countries at the end of 1991 (see Figure 4). IXI is one of the major
projects of COSINE (Cooperation for Open Systems Interconnection Networking in Europe). Although services have to be separately registered to
avoid overlap between national addressing schemes, access to IXI-linked networks from JANET is transparent. IXI carries now most non-X.400 mail,
and is expected soon to carry IP traffic within Europe. (See also below on the
European dimension to networking, TRIXI and on online searching.)

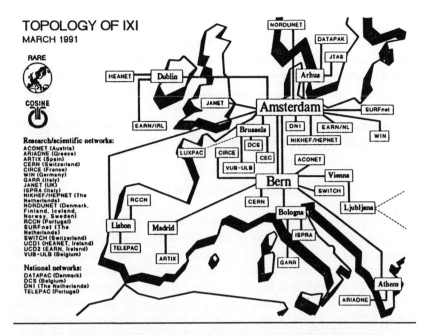

Current topology of IXI, March 1991. Adapted by Chris Ravilious from *DFN Mitteilungen.*

Figure 4. IXI: The European international X.25 infrastructure.

The PSS Gateway

There are currently three interlinked gateways to British Telecom's Public Packet SwitchStream (PSS) and its related international service, IPSS. (Note that BT has recently grouped its network services [including Tymnet] as Global Network Services [GNS].) The gateways carry calls both in and out of JANET. Use of PSS is charged on a volume basis and an account with the JNT for outgoing calls is required. Each gateway supports an interlinked accounting system and a uniform set of mnemonic names to set up connections.

Differences from the Internet for Librarians and Information Users

To users of the Internet, the central concepts will be familiar but there are considerable differences in detail. Users who login to a distant service, for example, an OPAC, do not "Telnet;" instead they make a "PAD" call, an acronym for the packet assembler disassembler software that packages asynchronous communications for the network. Blue Book file transfer works like TCP/IP FTP, but there is no widespread convention of "anonymous login" and therefore few "public" filestores. A major difference is the Name Registration Scheme (NRS) held centrally with its maintenance decentralized, and copied regularly to all services that require it. The numeric addresses attached to the NRS will change as each service makes the transition to OSI applications, but it is intended that the mnemonic service names will not be changed. Internet users should note that UK users conventionally cite addresses in an inverted order, putting the domain name (for example, UK.AC.) first.

Management, Funding, and Development

Use of the network is currently provided at no direct cost to individual users. The costs of operation are met by the major funding agencies for academic research and teaching, and by fixed annual charges to other organizations for connection. Institutions are responsible for the installation and management of their own network switches and routing equipment, though universities receive advice and financial assistance for standard installations from the Joint Network Team. Access to the network is normally granted without restriction to staff, and on request (though perhaps with some restrictions) to postgraduate and undergraduate students.

Policy for Computing in UK Higher Education and Research

Ten years ago, a very high proportion of funding for higher education and research in the United Kingdom was provided centrally; this has now been reduced. However, the larger part of non-fee income still derives from direct grants from the Universities Funding Council (the UFC) and the Polytechnics and Colleges Funding Council (PCFC). A proportion of the funds available to the UFC are disbursed, "top-sliced," to its sub-committee, the Information Systems Committee (ISC), previously the Computer Board for the Universities and Research Councils.

A major emphasis of this description of UK networking, written mainly for readers in the United States, has been to illustrate the benefits and problems of centralized funding and provide advice for UK networking. The main agent in this has been the Computer Board (at that time independent of the UFC), which at an early stage made conformance to agreed networking standards an essential requirement of all tenders. (This emphasis is also now found in the requirement within the European Community for all major computer installations to conform to OSI standards.) As a result, JANET and campus networks provided, by the mid-eighties, a very high standard of inter-working between most machines in academic institutions.

In 1991 the Computer Board lost some of its previous independence and became a subsidiary committee of the Universities Funding Council. At the same time its charge was increased to cover both administrative and library computing, and new members (for example, Derek Law, Librarian of King's College, London University) were appointed to represent these interests. However, within the year, a further restructuring of higher education was announced, abolishing the long-established distinction between universities and polytechnics, and decentralizing decision-making to new funding councils in England, Scotland, and Wales. A recent Government consultative paper has now brought the continuing role of the ISC into question: acknowledging a valuable role in (a) networking, (b) procurement, (c) software, (d) national initiatives, and (e) liaison and collaboration. It invites vice-chancellors and university principals to comment on the needs for a continuing central focus. Librarians were both pleased and apprehensive to see listed in this paper as important functions of the ISC (which may or may not continue), (a) liaison with the British Library and the UK Office for Library Networking, (b) development of information strategies, and (c) the central purchase and support of specialist datasets and information services.

The Management of JANET

The Network Advisory Committee (NAC) of the ISC acted until February 1992 as the main management committee of JANET. Previously chaired by Professor Harry Whitfield of Newcastle University, the current chairman is Professor Alistair Chalmers of the University of Sussex. Membership is drawn from each of the major funding councils who contribute to the operational costs of JANET, and also includes the current chairman of the JANET National User Group.

In the nine years since its inauguration, JANET has been funded from a variety of sources, and with an initially informal agreement on policy issues. The majority of its income has been from general funds for higher education, supplemented by contributions from each of the Research Councils, whose projects were major beneficiaries. As part of this arrangement the JNT has its offices at the Rutherford Appleton Laboratory, an establishment funded by the Science and Engineering Research Council. With the dramatic expansion of the range of networked applications not previously envisaged (for example, information dissemination by e-mail, or bibliographic record supply to libraries), the reduction in government funding for research and education, and the thriving demand for networking expertise and manpower, these initial arrangements needed to be reconsidered. In addition, it was important for the UK research and education community to establish a high-level formal framework for the development of all aspects of networking.

The outcome of these deliberations has been the establishment of the UK Educational and Research Networking Association (UKERNA, or more simply, The Association), whose objectives will be to increase the representation of academic and research interests, open up the network for industrial researchers, improve management and the establishment structure, obtain access to additional sources of funding, and seek industrial participation in collaborative projects. UKERNA will take on responsibility for the management of the network in April 1992. In February 1992 the functions of the Network Advisory Committee and the (Interim) Networking Policy Council (which established UKERNA) were combined in the Advisory Committee on Networking (ACN). Chaired by Professor Alistair Chalmers, this will report to the Universities Funding Council through its Information Systems Committee, and be broadly representative of all major interests.

Until its incorporation within UKERNA, JANET is managed and operated by the Joint Network Team (the JNT), based at the Rutherford Appleton Laboratory near Oxford. The JNT also has the major role in developing and approving ISC-funded applications for networking within academic institutions in the United Kingdom (see below). Of its staff, Dr. Robert Cooper is the director of networking, Dr. Willie Black is the head of the JNT, Dr. Ian Smith has responsibility for the operation of the JANET network, Dr. James Hutton (whom organizations wishing to connect should contact) is responsible for service, liaison and support, and Ms. Shirley Wood maintains close liaison with the library community. The JNT should be contacted in the first instance at the JANET-Liaison-Desk (see Figure 5).

The main information channel from the JNT is *Network News*, published three times a year, with a circulation of over 2,000. Articles are intended for a mainly technical readership and the acronym count is high.

JANET.News, the JNT-maintained bulletin board, provides interactive X.29 access and file transfer to a hierarchical set of text files: mainly directories and guides. There is little actual news, and no facilities for the exchange of information. The system software supporting this bulletin board is currently being replaced.

Topics on JANET.News include: network operational data; network addresses (Name Registration Scheme); gateway services (PSS, EARN, IXI); institutions and sites connected—details and contacts, help files and guides on mail, FTP, and other basic functions; reports of current projects and technical standards; lists of mail distribution lists; support services for UK computing (NISS, CHEST, CTISS); and reports and announcements from User Groups (see Figure 6).

```
>>> goto /networks/janet

GOTO completed
current path = /networks/janet

>>> info

INFO command completed
The result is in the body number : 2

----------------------------- Start of body part 2

JANET - UNITED KINGDOM

SECTION 1: NETWORK

Name of Network            : JANET
   Contact person/point    : Joint Network Team
   Postal address          : c/o Rutherford Appleton Laboratory,
                             Chilton, Didcot, Oxon, England.
                             OX11 0QX
   Telephone Number         : +44 235 445724
   Fax Number               : +44 235 33 5808
   E-mail address RFC822     : JNTSecretary@jnt.ac.uk
   E-mail address X.400      : c=GB;p=uk.ac;o=jnt;s=JNTSecretary

Extent of network:         : National
Scope of Network:          : Academic
                             General Research

Number of Institutions (universities,
colleges, research labs, companies etc)
connected to the Network     152 and increasing
Methods of access provided:
   Terminal logon
   File Transfer
   E-mail
   Job transfer
```

Figure 5. Contacting JANET: details from the CONCISE Help Service.

The JANET User Groups were established as an integral part of its management. The seven Regional User Groups meet normally three times a year, and each institution is invited to send both a member of their computing service staff, and a "real" user. To date only two Special Interest Groups exist, one for Particle Physics (which has a major requirement for data transfer and supercomputer access, and to support collaboration world-wide), and one for Libraries, of which more below. A SIG for University Administration may be set up in 1992. Two representatives from each group are invited to the JANET National User Group, which meets two or three times a year: the current chairman of JNUG is Michael Breaks, librarian of Heriot-Watt University, Edinburgh.

The User Groups do provide a useful channel to disseminate information on new developments and to sound opinion on the quality of new and

JANET.News and Index

```
PAD>call janet.news
```
%PAD-I-CONNECTED, Call connected

This is the JANET NEWS machine – log in with the id NEWS

Logging in
user `news`
ID last used Wednesday, 15 January 1992 12:17
Started – Wed 15 Jan 1992 12:18:27

Welcome to the JANET News Facility

If you have any comments or suggestions about this News facility please mail
them to POSTMASTER@JANET.NEWS
They will then be forwarded to the appropriate person for comment

Do you know how to use the VIEW command – Y or N – y

JANET.News Index

Filename	Contents
ADDRESS	List of Janet addresses in dte order.
CHEST	Information about CHEST (Combined Higher Education Software Team)
CONF	Information on conferences/workshops
CONTACTS	Networking Contacts for each Janet site (where known)
CTISS	Information about CTISS (Computers in Teaching Initiative Support Service)
DISTLIST	List of known distribution lists on JANET.
DOCUMENT	This file contains known document sources on JANET, as well as some documentation. The 'Beginners Guide to Janet' can be found in this catalogue.
DODAG	Technical Aspects of the Use of Internet Protocols to Support UK Academic Community Networking Interim Report of the JNT DoD Advisory Group
ETHER	Information on Ether components.
EUROKOM	Mail access to Eurokom.
EYP	Brief guide to BT's Electronic Yellow Pages.
FAULTS	Procedure to be taken when reporting a fault with JANET.
GATEWAYS	Information about the Network Executive supported Gateways on JANET – EAN, EARN and PSS.
etc.	

Figure 6. User group announcements and topics on JANET.News.

existing services. They allow a large number of people to participate, however vicariously, in an exciting venture. Several valuable projects have emerged from their enthusiasm, for example, the "Starter Pack" Project, the User Support Workshop, and from the JANET User Group for Libraries, the JUPITER Training Initiative. However, the meetings (and preparation for them) undoubtedly consume a great deal of JNT time: they also fail to attract a broad base of "real" discipline-based users (though local network intermediaries—user support staff and librarians—value them).

A major problem (true of all networks) of the users' perception of the efficiency of JANET is that the JNT and the Network Operation Teams tend to be blamed for unreliability in any remote services, whatever the cause. The management of JANET is itself in no way responsible for computer-based services provided by the individual institutions that are attached to it: its job is to ensure a reliable communications backbone. Clearly, a national networking strategy needs to be developed in close association with its potential users, though it is extremely unlikely that many of them will be interested in the underlying technical infrastructure. Few of the various academic associations and learned societies involved in coordinating subject-specific research in the United Kingdom have been forthcoming in proposing networked resources for their disciplines by user-group participation. A more direct approach is seen in Holland where the academic network, SURF, has an active program of subject-based user education and demonstrator projects.

The main annual network conference organized by the Joint Network Team for those working on the maintenance and development of the technical aspects of academic networking in the United Kingdom is Networkshop. Networkshop 19, 1991 was held at the University of Aberdeen, and Networkshop 20 on March 24-26, 1992 in the University of Leeds. The Proceedings were published soon after each conference, and consist of the OHPs used or abstracts of the presentations made. A limited number of copies are available from the JNT.

Networkshop 19 was attended by nearly 300 delegates and covered topics as diverse as full-screen services, multi-protocol networking, distance learning, industrial partnership, and security, and a wide range of projects and prototypes were on display.

Networkshop 20 had SuperJANET (see below) as its main theme, and papers covered the new technologies of ATM and SDH, multimedia networking, video conferencing, network publishing, and document delivery. Further papers discussed JIPS (the JANET IP service—see above) and the global Internet, archive servers, distributed filestores, CO/CL interworking, and WAN/LAN management. The change in management to UKERNA was reflected in policy papers on funding, and in broadening the community.

The themes of Networkshop are addressed in a Europe-wide context at the annual Joint European Networking Conference, organized by RARE, the Réseaux Associés pour la Recherche Européenne (the Association of European Research Networks). See the discussion below on European networking.

In September 1991, the JNT ran the first of an intended annual series of JANET User Support Workshops for staff of computing centers responsible for network user support. The concept had been proposed by the JANET National User Group, and followed the previous request for improved documentation that led to the "Starter" project. This first workshop was held at the University of Kent at Canterbury, and was planned to attract 50-60 people, but the final number attending was nearer 190. Topics discussed included access to other networks, support for collaborative research, the impact of X.500 directory services, early experience of user support for BIDS (the ISI database service at Bath University), the national subject-based user support program on SURFNet in Holland, and the "hot" topic of moving users from reliance on the EARN network. The proceedings have been published, and a summary of the recommendations appeared in *Network News*, 35, December 1991.

Current Projects and Developments

Planning for SuperJANET

At the time of this writing, the JANET Mark II upgrade, providing a 2mbps network to all main sites, is now largely in place. The "SuperJANET" project is the strategic development path for JANET over the next decade, creating a broadband wide-area network based on optical fiber technology. In contrast to the process of public lobbying in the United States to fund the NREN, the persuasion to fund SuperJANET has been almost discreet: a more cost-effective campaign perhaps but one that has so far not recruited the ranks of enthusiasts, nor an expectation of imaginative and futuristic services.

SuperJANET is expected to offer data transmission rates initially of hundreds of megabits per second, eventually gigabits per second using Asynchronous Transfer Mode (ATM) switching. SuperJANET will support video and voice transmission in addition to the traditional data communications: the advent of multimedia in which data, images, voice, and video can be integrated will be a key development. The project is intended to provide the major research test-bed for network developments within the United Kingdom and will seek participation from both central government and industrial sponsors. In November 1991 the Secretary of State for Education in his autumn financial statement announced initial funding of £5 million a year for three years for the project. No details are yet available.

Improvements to Electronic Mail Using OSI Standards (X.400 and X.500)

A major intended benefit of the transition to OSI mapped out in 1987 was the move from the "Grey Book" protocol for electronic mail to X.400. The present standard, like SMTP, is reliable and adequate for today's need for mail based on ASCII files, but does not provide the basis for carrying graphics, fax, and other images, nor for participating in the widely-shared vision of global message-based services, especially for EDI transactions within the commercial world. JANET now has a convertor for X.400 (1984) to Grey Book in service. However it is the later X.400 (1988) standard that is to be adopted within the UK academic community (to which International Standard members of the Joint Network Team have considerably contributed), and it is intended to deploy convertors on the network in early 1992. An X.400 (1988) gateway is now in service.

The X.500 directory protocol will provide access to a distributed database world-wide of information. The original purpose was to make it possible to identify mail addresses across the multitude of interlinked networks using X.400 electronic mail, and indeed the new mail systems will incorporate searching of the global database. However, it is obvious that this technology can be used (and misused) for maintaining and retrieving many forms of distributed information, for example, about people, about books, or about facilities and resources associated with a specific location or institution.

In 1989 the JNT sponsored the UK X.500 Directory Pilot to provide central support for this development, integral to an effective transition to X.400 mail. Within the United Kingdom, Directory Service Agents (DSAs) should be in operation in most universities by early 1992, providing around 60 service points out of a world total by then of over 200, and 60,000 directory entries out of a world total of over 300,000. X.500 is being promoted as part of the COSINE project and will be supported by Project PARADISE (see below).

The last example of projects supported by the Joint Network Team is on group communications: the GRACE project at the Communications Research Group of the University of Nottingham's Department of Computer Science. GRACE was primarily concerned to build on the emerging OSI communications standards (especially X.400 and X.500), to develop group communications tools in a distributed environment, for example, computer conferencing, activity management, help desk activities, structured enquiries, news control, pre- and post-moderation. The role of GRACE was primarily to provide input to emerging world standards and to prototype new systems.

The JNT Advisory Groups

The JNT, in its role of advising individual universities on all technical aspects of networking, both supports a range of advisory groups and funds projects to develop new applications. Much of its funding has for some years been distributed back to universities to contribute to the costs of installing and upgrading local campus networks. At the present time, there is a major initiative to assist with the installation of FDDI networks to provide 100mbps capacity on campus. The Lower Layers Group and others have been evaluating the alternatives for equipment, management, and operational standards.

The growth in the number of PCs has as yet not been met by commercially available software for OSI-based CONS networking. This is a major impediment to the adoption of OSI: there is as yet no terminal emulation and communications package comparable to the several "Windows"-based TCP/IP implementations. The JNT's PC-comms Group has contracted the development of "Rainbow" software to provide a uniform interface for PC networking, which incorporates Blue Book file transfer. In addition, Whitemail (so called since it incorporates all the coloured-book elements of the rainbow in its seven-layer OSI stack) is a PC implementation of an X.400 Mail User Agent. As a final example of a JNT advisory group, the CD-Networking Group was established following a successful seminar on CD-ROM networking. It will consider strategies for all forms of information delivery at the institutional level. Its charge is to consider CD-ROM networking, bulletin boards (CWISes), and menu-driven gateways to interactive services. Contact, for both groups, S.Weston@junt.uk.ac.

The "Starter Project:" Documentation for Connected Institutions

In late 1989 the JANET National User Group recommended that documentation on all main network services be brought up-to-date and made widely available. Many of the newly connected institutions were seeking straightforward advice as to how to make full and effective use of the network and others were transferring responsibility from their technical staff to their user support team. As a result the University of Sussex Computing Service contracted to gather or rewrite all the documentation, which is now available to institutions from the Joint Network Team. The full pack includes maps, staff responsibilities, network contacts, checklists for new institutions, details of all national services, the use of electronic mail, details of all network gateways, lots of examples, a list of documentation, and a glossary. The text of some of the documentation (the "Starter Card," for example) is held online on the bulletin board service JANET.News.

While this documentation is invaluable, it is not written for the general user, but for user support staff of the computing service on each campus. With the exception of SURFnet, most national research networks fail to provide any general advice, publicity, training, or news of potential uses. (A recent survey of user support in Europe has been compiled by Jill Foster for the RARE Working Group 3 on Information Services.) Although it is argued that the undocumentable range of local variations make central guidance and promotion impossible, librarians and others have found a steady demand for popular basic training.

Participation in European Networking

It is clear from the descriptions above that the development of JANET is closely integrated within an emerging pan-European framework. The main initiative comes from EUREKA Project No. 8, COSINE, Cooperation for Open Systems Interconnection Networking in Europe. This is funded by 18 European countries, as well as the Commission of the European Communities (CEC). Its main purpose is to create a computer networking infrastructure, based on the use of OSI protocols, which will provide services to the research and development community throughout Europe. It aims to extend the types of data communications and messaging facilities to the whole of Europe in a systematic and consistent manner. Although the project is technically ambitious in terms of its support for a next generation of communications structures, it lacks the funding, authority, and the vision needed to achieve a European NREN.

The COSINE contract is managed by RARE, the Réseaux Associés pour la Recherche Européenne, and the project is divided into a number of sub-projects and services. These include the IXI (International X.25 Infrastructure) backbone network, the proposed 2mbps fiber-optic EMPP link (European Multi-protocol Pilot Project) between the United Kingdom, Germany, Switzerland, CERN, and possibly France and Italy, pilot gateway services to the United States (including an FTAM gateway), support of typical international usergroups, migration strategies to OSI, diagnostic network management tools and accounting mechanisms, demonstrations and equipment procurement exercises, and security mechanisms. A growing range of services are now available including Europe-wide IP access (the European backbone), access to EARN, and X.400 electronic mail.

RARE and the COSINE Project Management Unit can be contacted at The RARE Secretariat, Singel 466-468, NL-1017 AW Amsterdam; and by electronic mail at raresec@rare.nl, by fax at +31 20 6391131, and by telephone at +31 20 6391131.

Two major projects for COSINE are being developed within the UK. PARADISE (Piloting A ReseArchers' DIrectory Service for Europe) is intended to provide the core infrastructure for X.500 on the European networks. The project is based at the Department of Computer Science, University College, London, and has as objectives to establish a Europe-wide X.500 pilot directory service for a community of over 500,000 researchers, and to co-ordinate the several national directory pilots (on INRIA [France], DFN [Germany], SURFNet [Netherlands], SUNET [Sweden], FUNET [Finland], UNINET [Norway], and JANET [United Kingdom]). Contact: helpdesk@paradise.ulcc.ac.uk.

CONCISE (COsine Network's Central Information Service for Europe) aims to provide a pilot pan-European information service to the Europe-

---

The **COsine Network's Central Information Service for Europe** –
a pilot pan-European information service for the research community, and a central
focal point for national networks.

Topics stored on the server are:

projects	conferences and meetings
COSINE	network products
special interest groups	networks

Information on national network services:

other information services	directories
distribution list servers	file servers
conference servers	database servers
super computers	service machines
bulletin boards	gateways, relays and converters
special computing facilities	other resources & servers

The User Guide is available:

mail   helpdesk@concise.level-7.co.uk
with the message start
                     help user-guide

CONCISE,   Fax +44 344 868442 Phone +44 344 360049
Level-7 Ltd,   Centennial Court, Easthampstead Road,
                     Bracknell, Berkshire, RG12 1YQ, UK

Figure 7. The COSINE Network Information Service—CONCISE.

an research community, based on an open system environment and accessible
by OSI protocols. It will complement national network information services
(see Figures 7 and 8).

The Joint European Networking Conference, the main annual conference for members of RARE, COSINE project members, and associates is
held each year in May: in 1990 in Killarney, Eire; in 1991, in Blois, France;
and in 1992 in Innsbruck, Austria. Each year several themes are run in paral-
lel. The advance program is available by electronic mail, and the proceedings
for the first two conferences have been published by Elsevier in *Computer
Networks and ISDN Systems*. Contact raresec@nikhef.nl.

The *DG XIII magazine*, replacing *I'M* and *IES News*, provides a general overview of telecommunications development within the countries of the
European community. The editorial content is directed mainly at policy mak-
ers. Other than the information within CONCISE (and certain formal policy
statements), there is little general publicity about most individual projects, or
of the potential of the COSINE initiative for stimulating collaboration and
communication across Europe.

This category covers electronic services available over the European networks. The services may be of any type; typically they are information servers, bulletin boards, electronic mail list servers, databases, and conference servers. All services are available to the academic and research community in Europe. Some may be free to use; some have to be paid for by the users.

aconetdir	Directory service for Graz University, Austria
brunet	OPAC at the University of Utrecht
caos-camm	Chemical research tools
celex	Lexical database on language and speech
cosine-mhs	Information about COSINE-MHS project
dfndir	German Directory Service
dfninfo	DFN Information System
earn-sw	EARN/BITNET user services
ethics	Catalog federal Institute Technology in Zurich
excerpta	Humanities and social science service.
frlistserv	EARN France List server
janetnews	Networking information on JANET
macserve	Filestore of public-domain Mac software
netnews	EARN France Bulletin Board
netserv	Programs and information about EARN/BITNET
niss	UK Info Software Services Bulletin Board
npdsa	UK national Public Domain Software Archive
qom	DFN Conference System QOM
redirisdir	Spanish Directory Service
redirisdoc	RedIRIS Documentation
se-master	Directory server for Sweden
searn	Swedish List and File server
srm	Social science database
surfbull	Surfnet Bulletin
surfis	Dutch national information service
surfnetdoc	Guide through SURFnet
sw-netserv	Swedish file-server
switchdb	Swiss Database service
switchinfo	Information about the COSINE-MHS project
swlib and swlibcoll	Library catalogue of University of Zuerich
trickle	File server about micro-computer programs
yunameserv	Yugoslavian nameserver
zurichinf	Information service about the University Zurich

Figure 8. CONCISE services index.

The Development of Applications and Information Services
on the Network

The implicit objectives of any wide-area academic network like JANET are to support collaboration in research and teaching, enable sharing of resources, and improve access to information. Kenneth King, president of EDUCOM, in proposing objectives for the U.S. NREN, described them as:

- to share (inter)nationally scarce or centralized resources

- to distribute experimental work, data collection, and theory-building throughout the academic community

- to support collaboration between distant institutions

- to deliver information to the workplace: the laboratory, classroom, desk, office—or home

- to contribute to the research community's information resource.

The Central Role of the Information Systems Committee

The ISC (and its predecessor the Computer Board) has not only been responsible for funding University computing and networking: it has increasingly involved itself with provision of software and datasets, all aspects of training, and most important, in encouraging an "information systems policy" on each campus. The following are but some examples of these policies.

The Nelson Report of 1983 identified at an early date the need for equipment, software, and skilled manpower for use in teaching. As a result, the Computers in Teaching Initiative (CTI), established in 1985, aimed to promote a greater awareness of the potential of information technology in teaching, to facilitate the development of skills, to encourage the development of computer-assisted teaching, and to evaluate hardware, software, and organizational requirements. The first program funded 139 pilot projects in all subjects, and the second, current, program has established 20 subject-based coordination centers responsible for disseminating information on appropriate software and services (see Figure 9). The CTI centers all produce newsletters, contribute to the NISS Bulletin Board, produce guides to software and information sources, and disseminate information through conferences and articles. CTISS, coordinating the work of the centers, publishes regular overviews in *The CTISS File*.

Subject	University
Accountancy (with Finance & Business Studies)	East Anglia
Biology	Liverpool
Chemistry	Liverpool
Computing	Ulster
Economics	Bristol
Engineering	QMW, London
Geography (with Geology)	Leicester
History	Glasgow
Human Services	Southampton
Land Use	Aberdeen
Law	Warwick
Library & Information Studies	Loughborough
Mathematics/Statistics	Birmingham/Glasgow
Medicine	Bristol
Modern Languages (with Classics)	Hull
Music	Lancaster
Physics	Surrey
Psychology	York
Sociology & Social Policy (with Politics)	Stirling
Textual Studies	Oxford
CTISS	Oxford

Figure 9. Computers in Teaching Initiative (CTI) Centers.

More recently in 1991 the ISC funded the Information Technology Training Initiative (ITTI) to improve the availability of training materials specifically for information technology. Twenty-two projects have been funded for systems to train in the use of, for example, multimedia, geographical information systems, relational databases, computer graphics, and UNIX.

The success of BIDS (see below) and the growing demand for coordinated provision or purchasing of datasets and text databases led to the establishment of the National Datasets Working Party in 1990. In practice, the Board and the Research Councils had been funding datasets for some years as primary data for research purposes (see Figure 12 for some examples). But the information became easier to manipulate making it more usable (for example, full text replacing brief indexes), and was applied to undergraduate teaching thanks to the quality of spreadsheets and other PC software. The Working Party recognized the value of an overall policy to manage central assistance and coordination with purchasing, the need to fund "hosts" (the computer platforms needed to mount the services), and the potential of the network to distribute access. The report of the Working Party was not considered by the Computer Board before its demise, and thus a potentially invaluable national initiative for central support for networked information provision was allowed to lapse. The topic has not been considered by the newly born ISC, though it is mentioned in the discussion paper of its continuing role. In the meantime, the expectation of a coherent national policy may have inhibited plans at individual universities.

The last example is the Management and Administrative Computing initiative (Project MAC). The complexity of systems requirements for administrative computing in a time of rapid expansion of access to higher education—though not of funding—has led to the creation by the UFC of a limited number of "families" to develop management systems based on the relational databases, Oracle, Ingres, and Powerhouse. This work is now coordinated by the ISC. The relatively standard specifications will enable a uniform approach to statistical reporting, the implementation of PC-based SQL applications, and closer integration of, for example, student records with the national Clearinghouses for admissions, or budgeting with library acquisitions systems. In late 1991, informal proposals were made for a complementary initiative to encourage a greater degree of standard functionality for library systems.

The Representative Role of the Inter-University Committee on Computing

The computing services of the universities in the United Kingdom are all members of the IUCC, which is firmly established as a coordinating agency with government bodies such as the Universities Funding Council, the ISC, the Central Computing and Telecommunications Agency (CCTA), and the Research Councils. Much of the work of the committee is carried on through its sub-committees, notably the Inter-University Software Committee (IUSC) which works closely with CHEST (see below) to negotiate software pricing, the Inter-University Network Committee (IUNC) which liaises with the JNT over the use of JANET and the provision of campus networking, the Inter-University Information Committee (IUIC) coordinating user support and information, and, fourth, the Inter-University Training Committee (IUTC) working in collaboration with the ITTI (see above) and the Committee of Vice Chancellors and Principals Staff Development and Training Unit. With such a large proportion of decision-making and funding in computing matters carried out centrally, the level of participation and activity of these committees is not surprising. In contrast, university libraries attract little attention from the Universities Funding Council, and the librarians show less willingness to coordinate policy within their national body, SCONUL.

The disadvantages of well-intentioned national and regional planning have been very visible in recent years, and enthusiasts for deregulation criticize the dependency of mind that they say has resulted in individual universities from the Computer Board's positive initiatives and robust insistence on standards. But the converse, the freedom of libraries to act individually, has resulted in five or more utilities delivering bibliographic records, no national database or guide to resources, a lack of file transfer and e-mail on many library systems, little collaborative software development, and a national library outside the general communications and information handling framework of its academic community.

Currently Available National Services

The National Information on Software and Services Project (NISS) was established in 1988 as a joint project at the Universities of Bath and Southampton. It received initial funding from the then Computer Board and has attracted further support from ICL, IBM, Hewlett-Packard, Dell, DEC, and most recently, SUN. NISS provides a valued information gateway (see Figure 10) from which several services can be called, such as the online hosts STN in Germany (providing for example Chemical Abstracts), the National Public Domain Software Archive, and, in early 1992, several major U.S. campus services, using JIPS for direct Internet access.

They also maintain the online NISS bulletin board (NISSBB), which is a focal point for computer-related information on JANET (see Figure 11). Topics covered include current prices and latest details of all software available through CHEST, information on the Computers in Teaching and many JANET-related projects, conference reports and committee minutes of many computing interest groups. Contact NISS@bath.ac.uk.

The gateway also provides access to the NISS Public Access Collection (NISSPAC), a networked OPAC of software and datasets at UK higher education institutions. This also contains details of the IBM Study Contracts, VAX/VMS applications software, public domain software for PCs and Macs, and text-based data collections. Contact: NISS@ibm.soton.ac.uk.

Closely associated with NISS and also based at Bath University, the Combined Higher Education Software Team (CHEST) aims to negotiate prices and license terms for the use of commercial software within the UK higher education and research community. While CHEST facilitates, administers, and advises on licensing the use of software on behalf of the community, it relies on expert working parties (usually set up by the IUSC) to evaluate products and make recommendations. Major software deals negotiated by

NISS (National Information on Software and Services)

```
The

  |**|    |*|      |*|    |******|    |******|
  |*|*|   |*|      |*|    |*|         |*|
  |*||*||*|        |*|    |******|    |******|
  |*|  |*|*|       |*|         |*|         |*|
  |*|    |**|      |*|    |******|    |******|   Gateway
```

A :)   NISSBB – The NISS Bulletin Board

B :)   NISSPAC – The NISS Public Access Collections

E :)   Information Services in Europe

U :)   Information Services in the UK

H :)   Help Information / NEWS

X,Q :)   Logoff the Gateway

Please select your option (A, B, E, H, U, X or Q)

Figure 10. NISS provides a valued information gateway.

CHEST, now all widely used in British universities, include UNIRAS (graphics), the NAG Library (of numerical algorithms), SPSS-PC (statistical analysis), BRS/Search (text retrieval), Oracle and Ingres (relational databases), well-known PC packages and many more. A standard Code of Conduct for the use of software bought through CHEST is in force. The CHEST Software Directory is printed annually and also on the NISS Bulletin Board. Contact CHEST@Bath.ac.uk.

CHEST also negotiated the purchase and continuing provision for five years of the entire database of the Institute of Scientific Information (ISI)—familiar to all students and researchers as the various Citation Indexes and Current Contents. BIDS, the Bath Information and Data Services, provides an online open access network service to this database for all staff and students on over 50 subscribing campuses. In six months, BIDS grew to be the world's largest ISI service. There are plans under discussion to extend the scope of service to users (similar to CARL in the United States) to include document delivery from the British Library's Document Supply Service. Contact BIDS@Bath.ac.uk.

The four major Research Councils in the UK, the Science and Engineering Research Council (SERC), the Economic and Social Research Council (ESRC), the Natural Environment Research Council (NERC), and the

```
┌──────────────────────────────────────────────────────────────────┐
│ Section M                                             Page   1 of  1 │
│                                                                    │
│        ::::: NISS BULLETIN BOARD ::::::: MAIN MENU :::::            │
│                                                                    │
│  A   INTRO. for New Users & Contributors      ACADEMIC DISCIPLINES │
│  B   NISS Public Access                 N   Accountancy to Engineer.│
│      Collections(NISSPAC)                                          │
│  C   Academic Computer Services         O   Geography to Literature │
│  D   Software/Information Services       P   Maths. to Physics       │
│      (CHEST, CTISS, NPDSA etc.)         R   Statistics to Sociology │
│  E   Library Services                                              │
│  F   Online Information Sources                                    │
│  G   Job Vacancies                      M   MAIN MENU              │
│  H   Computing Groups and Committees     S   Computer Supplier      │
│                                             Information            │
│  I   Subject INDEX                      T   Research Councils       │
│  J   Special Interest Groups            X   Latest CHANGES *        │
│  K   Training Courses, Workshops, etc.   Y   Public Pinboard        │
│  L   Joint Academic NETwork (JANET)     Z   Table of CONTENTS       │
│                                                                    │
│   ::::: Section K, covering Meetings, Conferences, Workshops, Training ::::: │
│   ::::: has been reorganised. See Section A7 for more details.      ::::: │
│   :::::                                                       ::::: │
│                                                                    │
│  Options:   HELP HINTS SEARCH MAIL POST QUIT M (Main Menu)          │
│             or <RETURN> (Next Page)                                │
│             Please select section name, page number, or option:    │
└──────────────────────────────────────────────────────────────────┘
```

Figure 11. The NISS Bulletin Board.

Medical Research Council (MRC), as well as the British Academy and the British Library, have all encouraged in various ways the provision of datasets accessible across the JANET network. Some of these were sited at a set of Regional Computer centers; others are available from major laboratories and funded institutes. For example, the Oxford University Computing Service maintains the Oxford Text Archive as one of several projects associated with the humanities. Its catalog can be searched online on the humanities bulletin board, HUMBUL, based at Oxford and also available in the United States by mail as one of the Humanist services from LISTSERV@BROWNVM. At the University of Essex the ESRC Data Archive combines both primary data from funded fellowships and major public sets. Sample data sets are the UK

Bath University
  Census data, 1981
  Meteorological data for the South West
  CSO time series data
  OECD overseas trade statistics
  EXSTAT financial data on 3000
  companies
  World bank world tables
	University of Manchester
	  Central Statistical Office. Time
	  series data
	  UNIDO industrial statistics
	  OECD economic indicators
	  EMBL nucleotide sequences
	  PIR protein sequences
	  Cambridge structure database

Daresbury laboratory
  Chemical databank
	Newcastle University
	  Census data, 1981

Durham University
  Employment statistics
	Oxford University
	  Oxford Text Archive

Essex University
  ESRC Data Archive
	Rutherford Appleton laboratory
	  Solar terrestrial physics
	  Geophysical data

London, Queen Mary College
  CRONOS time series data
  Central Statistical Office data
	Wind energy: meteorological data

Figure 12. Statistical and numerical datasets networked in the United Kingdom.

Population Census (1851), 1966, 1971, 1981, and other national census data, Opinion Polls, Trade and Industry Statistics, and EEC National Labour Force Surveys.

The value of data derived from the decennial UK Censuses of Population and other social surveys has increased with the availability of digitized map data, and geographic and other analytical tools designed to manipulate the information. In the early 1980s, major subsets of the 1981 census were made available at the major regional computing centers. In late 1991, the ISC, in collaboration with the Economic and Social Research Council, commissioned a £3 million project to develop the use of the 1991 Census of Population. This project includes (a) the purchase of the Small Areas Statistics (SAS) data, (b) a support and dissemination service for a sample of anonymized records, (c) exploitation of the Longitudinal Study data and, (d) digitization of census electoral district boundaries. This, coupled with a major training program, is expected to have considerable impact on the practice and teaching of social and demographic analysis.

The most popular information service on the network is the National Public Domain Software Archive (NPDSA) based at Lancaster University (pdsoft@pdsoft.lancs.ac.uk) and funded by the ISC. The archive contains a large collection of public domain and shareware material available to the community for all popular makes of personal computers. It also acts as the UK distribution center for Kermit file transfer implementations. Software can be retrieved interactively, by mail, or file transfer.

The last example of national support for information dissemination on JANET is the Networked Information Services Project (NISP) based at the University of Newcastle. Most of the traffic on today's networks is electronic mail, and most electronic mail will have been generated by one of the many distribution list systems that are available. Such distributed electronic mail has become perhaps the main news and information channel for network users. Although most mail systems can distribute mail to a list of addresses compiled by the sender, such lists are difficult to maintain and require constant attention. In contrast, the LISTSERV software, originally devised for IBM machines on BITNET and EARN, enables users to subscribe and unsubscribe themselves, provides facilities for a "moderator" to scan incoming mail before its redistribution, and enables users to retrieve lists of other subscribers, archives of past messages, and files that have been saved to the list's own file-store. These facilities combine to provide a very flexible framework for communications within an interest group.

In 1989 Jill Foster of the University of Newcastle upon Tyne put forward a proposal for NISP and to develop Mailbase, an application similar to LISTSERV but capable of running on X.25 networks using a standard UNIX platform and widely available software. In addition, the specification provided for interactive access to the database. By the end of the initial two-year project, ten different groups were using the pilot system, running 55 different lists, to a total of nearly 2,000 distinct users, many of whom subscribed to two or more lists. The project has been renewed, as NISP II, to provide a central service (with the software available to other sites at a later date), to improve the interactive interface and add free text retrieval capability, and especially to help, encourage, and train special user groups to use the service. The emphasis now is above all on user group support. NISP is funded by the ISC through the JNT. The project team can be contacted at nisp-team@Newcastle.ac.uk.

Developments at Individual Universities

This review of JANET has deliberately concentrated on the development of a national infrastructure for networking and information handling. It has therefore underemphasized the very considerable contribution made by individuals and specific institutions in sharing what previously could be provided but locally. Networks enable us to harness resources that are widely scattered, and allow us to make our own contribution to the common good, distance is no barrier and the role of the center (of government or funding agency, etc.) becomes one of coordination rather than of command. Librarians and archivists, for centuries controllers of the access to knowledge, are now having to set up their information stalls along the global highway.

Exactly how users will find their way through the diversity of electronic material available is far from understood; what is the ideal format of a network resource guide? NISS for the United Kingdom, and CONCISE for the European networks, currently provide the main centrally-funded pointers, and there are a handful of guides produced by individual enthusiasts. However, as yet there is little structure to support specific disciplines and subject areas of study. The IUIC Working Group on Information Services (previously known as SAGE) maintains a watching brief, and is coordinating the spread of CWISs and information gateways on campuses.

Use of JANET by Libraries

Libraries and Access to JANET

Since JANET was conceived as a network to link all institutions of higher education and research (and not—like SERCnet and ARPAnet—to provide research grant holders with shared facilities), and because there was some central subsidy of general purpose campus networks, the libraries of these institutions were very quickly in a position to make use of the network. Indeed, they did so sooner than their North American counterparts and were only held back by the cost of the additional terminals, personal computers, and other building-specific equipment.

The financial benefit of using JANET to send interlibrary loan requests to BLDSC or for online searching, and the popularity of a campuswide OPAC, was immediately attractive. Only the polytechnics, who received no inducement to install standard network infrastructure on their campuses, delayed in connecting their libraries. The reform of higher education in 1989, a process which re-starts in 1992, provided a more coherent national structure. In 1991 the costs of maintaining links, now to an even larger number of colleges, were shared out centrally.

Several major libraries not funded by the Department of Education and Science now fund their own connection: the National Libraries of Scotland and Wales, and the British Library (which, of course, through its ARTtel and BLAISE services receives considerable revenue from the academic sector). Unfortunately, these independent connections rarely support the full range of services normally available (file transfer, mail). Nor do they have a substantial local community that needs a wide range of general computing facilities. Several of the British Library staff have been provided with a mailbox at the JNT headquarters, although most of the BL departments have remained electronically *incommunicado*, unable to satisfy a world-wide demand for their services and expertise.

To create a true framework for all non-commercial research libraries in the UK, it would be necessary to connect several other major independent collections, for example, the National Art Library and the private London Library, and to link the major local authority-maintained public libraries, as well as the library services attached to government ministries and all those which support the health services. The expense of connecting these libraries to offer their services is currently too high. The present physical structure of JANET is based on the provision of relatively high-capacity X.25 leased lines over fairly long distances to one of the eight Network Operation Centres, the annual cost of which, at approximately £10K, outweighs the probable benefits. If JANET is to facilitate communications to and encompass all of the major academic resources of the United Kingdom, then low-cost local connections, perhaps to neighboring universities, need to be encouraged. The matter is currently under review.

The JANET User Group for Libraries (JUGL)

The use of JANET by libraries is kept under review by the JANET User Group for Libraries (JUGL), which works closely with both the Joint Network Team and the National User Group. JUGL has run several workshops and conferences for librarians, produces directories and the *JUGL Newsletter* and initiated the training program for libraries, Project JUPITER, funded by the UGC and based at Glasgow University Library.

JUGL was brought into being by a direct invitation in 1986 to the representative committees of University Librarians (SCONUL) and Polytechnic Librarians (COPOL) from Prof. Mike Wells (since the mid-1970s, the main proponent of a national network strategy in the United Kingdom, professor of computing at the University of Leeds, and director of networking for the JNT, 1984-1988). Membership in JUGL is automatic for any library eligible to connect, and a new committee is elected annually. JUGL has considerably extended its original brief of commenting on the quality of the network service, has proselytized with vigor, run workshops and gained funding for more, lobbied widely, and is often cited as a good example of effective self-interest. In 1990 it was awarded the Robinson Medal of the Library Association for technical innovation. The current chair is Frances Krivine of Aston University, Birmingham (krivinehf@aston.ac.uk).

The formal objectives of JUGL are defined in the policy statement reproduced in Figure 13. Informally, there have been two major achieve-

JANET USER GROUP FOR LIBRARIES Policy Statement, 24.4.91

'The JANET User Group for Libraries (JUGL) encourages the use of the Joint Academic NETwork (JANET) by libraries and their users, acts as a forum for the discussion of their use of the network, and makes proposals for its further development. It aims to assist in the development and training of the library profession in the effective use of the network, and promotes standards and service objectives for new forms of information dissemination.'

Objectives

- Network service quality for library activities
  - to provide a forum for any matters of concern to JANET users in libraries
- Information services
  - to promote the development of networked information
  - to support initiatives to raise awareness of available networked services both national and international
- Information systems design
  - to press for the adoption of open standards by library system suppliers
  - to advise on the profiles of library requirements for applications
  - to provide a forum for the development of initiatives and demonstrations of library networking applications, distributed services, etc
  - to consider and advise on the coordination of requirements and funding for specific library and information services within the academic community
- User support
  - to encourage support for users of networked information services across JANET
  - to encourage the production of documentation to assist libraries in the use of JANET
- Development and training
  - to encourage training initiatives
  - to encourage awareness of JANET among departments of and information studies
- Liaison with the Joint Network Team (JNT)
  - to make representations to the JNT over quality, price, conditions and extension of JANET connections
  - to work through the JANET National User Group (JNUG) for the improvement of services to users
  - to monitor access to relevant services on other networks and their gateways
- External representation and liaison
  - to make formal and informal representation of users' views to all relevant bodies
  - to liaise with other national and/or international bodies
  - to maintain contact with user groups for library services on academic networks nationally and internationally
  - to promote the use of JANET at relevant conferences and exhibitions

The use of the JANET Network by libraries is intended to lead to improvements in all forms of communication between libraries, their suppliers and their users; in the acquisition of books and periodicals, and the supply of loans and photocopies between libraries within the UK and internationally; and in access to information in electronic forms on behalf of and by library users.

Figure 13. JUGL's formal objectives.

ments. The first has been the creation of an active community of network users among library staff: the result of many workshops run by committee enthusiasts (and later by Project JUPITER) and of the regular compilation and distribution of a directory of the electronic mail addresses of all the libraries, their major services and staff. These activities have been backed up by an annual conference and the quarterly *JUGL Newsletter*.

The second has been to raise the image of librarians as major stakeholders in determining network policy. The status of any User Group is as high as the quality of advice it gives. JUGL has twice put forward project proposals that have been accepted. When the University Grants Committee in 1987 requested bids from individual universities to improve the communications aspects of library services, JUGL made a proposal for the JUPITER project. This training program ran for two years, based at Glasgow University Library, and provided a series of workshops, produced a full guide and training manual and established BUBL, the Bulletin Board for Libraries (see Figure 14).

JUGL had always been aware that the United Kingdom lacked a proper national framework for the development of library and information networking compared with the coherent overall planning in most European countries but that it represented only the libraries of academic institutions. Following an approach to the British Library, the UK Office for Library Networking (UKOLN) was established at the University of Bath to provide a representative forum for the development of library networking. UKOLN is currently running a series of two-day conferences to determine a common and cohesive strategy for networking among all groups of libraries and in collaboration with the book trade and system suppliers. In April 1992, UKOLN hosted a conference on networking and the future of libraries to focus on strategic and policy issues.

The extensive use of electronic mail by libraries is touched on at various points in this review. The e-mail directory *JANET-Libmail* contained 20 pages of names and services in mid-1991 and provided an address for all but a handful of the libraries known to be eligible to use the network. Nearly 700 subscribe to the mailing list *LIS-Link@newcastle.ac.uk* for general news and information.

The number of networked e-mail services continues to grow steadily. From 1986 till 1990, a single mailing list (now defunct), *library_mailing@rl*, was used to distribute messages to a single mailbox in each library, which led to the widespread adoption of *library* as the standard mailname on each campus. The NISP project (see above) provided the opportunity to develop a wide range of distribution lists which required somewhat less maintenance. UK librarians are not nearly as communicative as their American colleagues and some lists have now been closed. Nonetheless, NISP supports LIS-Link, LIS-Enquiries, LIS-ILL, LIS-Scotland, LIS-

---

bubl bubl bubl bubl bubl bubl bubl bubl

Welcome to BUBL, the 'Bulletin Board for Libraries'. BUBL is an electronic Bulletin Board set up originally under Project Jupiter, and now maintained by a team of volunteers based mainly at the two universities in Glasgow.

BUBL is designed specifically to host information of interest to JANET-using librarians, and suggestions for the inclusion of new items are always welcome. Contact: Dennis Nicholson (cijs03@uk.ac.strathclyde.vaxa) or Chris Bailey (c.bailey@uk.ac.glasgow.cms)

UPDATES: Regular bulletins are sent out via LIS-link, which is also the forum for discussions about BUBL (details Section A2).
This service is running the USERBUL Software, copyright Leicester University.

Press the Return key to proceed to the Main Menu :

Section M   Page 1 of 1

*****MAIN MENU*****

A	All about BUBL	J	Glossary
B	Reference Section	K	Practical exercises
C	New titles in LIS	L	British Library R &D News
D	Directories	** N	Latest changes to BUBL
E	Current Contents	O	CONCISE (Pan-European Inf.Serv.)
F	Mailing lists	S	Electronic Journals & Texts
G	NISS	V	Library Systems & Software
H	Users' board	Z	CTILIS

Options: HELP HINTS SEARCH MAIL POST QUIT M (Main Menu) or
<RETURN> (Next Page)
Please select section name, page number or option :

Figure 14. BUBL, the Bulletin Board for Libraries.

Medical, LIS-Rarebooks, LIS-X500, LIS-SCONUL, LIS-Geac, LIS-Research, all @mailbase.ac.uk. Those open for general subscription can be joined by sending a message to Mailbase@mailbase.ac.uk with the single line message: subscribe <listname> <firstname> <surname>, as for any LIST-SERV list on BITNET.

In 1986, in the enthusiasm for electronic communication, a group of polytechnic and university librarians created a mail group, COPOST, within British Telecom's Dialcom/Telecom Gold service. This was done specifically to include those with poor campus connectivity and to exchange mail with libraries and suppliers outside the academic community, and on the understanding that interworking with JANET would soon be possible. In 1988, the Library Association took on this service as LANET. The promised internetwork e-mail service finally became available in 1991, by which time X.400 messaging from other networks was becoming common.

Finally, BUBL, the Bulletin Board for Libraries, started originally by Project JUPITER, was taken on by Dennis Nicholson and others in the Universities of Strathclyde and Glasgow in mid-1991. It has recently expanded its coverage to include all the major library resource guides, abstracts, and indexes to library science journals, information on grants and conferences, and much more (see Figure 14). Contact d.m.nicholson@vaxa.strathclyde.ac.uk.

Interlibrary Lending and Document Supply

The pattern of document supply in the United Kingdom is substantially different from that of many other countries. The role of the British Library's Document Supply Center (BLDSC) is central: academic libraries address probably 80 percent of their requests to BLDSC in the first instance. Many public libraries do work primarily within regional interlending systems and many medical libraries (both within the academic community and outside) do collaborate closely. However, for universities and polytechnics, BLDSC is the main provider of journal articles and ARTtel its main channel.

The BLDSC ARTtel system was connected to JANET in 1987, although it had been accessible over the public network since 1984, and indeed derives from the long-standing telex-based ARTtel service. The requesting library will prepare a text file of requests (normally in ARTtel's quaint uppercase and 40-character line mode with no punctuation), login to BL.BLAISE across the network, and "upload" the text file. There is no provision for interactive file preparation, nor conventional network file transfer, nor for receiving reports or requests by electronic mail. In late 1991 BLDSC announced that it would accept enquiries of its customer support division by e-mail to BLDSC@jnt.ac.uk.

Interlending between libraries has made more effective use of electronic mail. Most ILL departments have their own mailbox, most are members of the Forum for Interlending (FIL), which has published guidelines for e-mail requests, and most subscribe to their own mailing list, LIS-ILL@ncl.ac.uk.

Major developments in the near future might be expected from the imminent connection of LASER, formally the London and South-East Region Interlending Cooperative. LASER has an impressive track record of innovation and experimentation. Although its services have to date been used primarily by public libraries, this is likely to change. LASER is a co-partner in the European Community-funded Project ION (Interlending OSI Network) with the Dutch library cooperative, PICA, and the French library framework, SUNIST. The Dutch and French partners consist of mainly academic libraries. The project will use X.400 protocols and interactive services, and hopes to facilitate international library exchange.

Finally, BLDSC and the JNT have been considering the potential of the high capacity of JANET II and the SuperJANET network for direct delivery of full text and page images of requested documents.

OPACs

Over 70 OPACs of almost all British university and polytechnic libraries, and of certain specialist services (such as the Institute of Terrestrial Ecology and the NISSPAC catalog of datasets and software) are now accessible across JANET (see Figure 15). They have all been registered for use across the X.25 IXI network in Europe, and can be accessed through the NSFNet-Relay from the Internet. Since JANET is connected to the public PSS network—British Telecom's Global Network Service—they are, in effect, fully public services.

A directory, *JANET-OPACS*, has been maintained since 1986 by the University of Sussex Library. It is available, in a machine-readable form, on all the main UK Bulletin Boards (BUBL, NISSBB, and JANET.News), in Billy Baron's and Art St. George's Internet guides, on Peter Scott's HYTEL-NET, and, printed, from the University of Sussex (Library@central.Sussex.ac.uk).

Despite the availability of so many catalogs as early as 1986, little has been done yet to make them either more accessible or more useful to the community as a whole. The British Library funded a project, SALBIN, to develop PC software to call up OPACs (to support inter-institutional collaboration in Scotland), and this software is available from the NPDSA service. Hull University Library offers network access to all as part of the Library OPAC and records over 1,000 sessions a week. But overall, there are few campus information gateways offering access from a menu, and few of the OPACs offer services, beyond simple lookup, of use to remote enquirers. Remote users should at least be able to leave messages, or queries, and be able to select a set of items as a downloaded list, not as a sequence of screen images full of prompts. Ideally, they should be able to initiate a search across a sequence of libraries, retrieve information about appropriate items when a match is found and use it later to request loans.

An interesting bibliographic service, not online but based on electronic mail, was developed at the University of Sussex and has since been im-

JANET-OPACS
Online public access catalogues in the UK

compiled for JUGL by the University of Sussex Library, 30 January 1992
(Available on all main network resource guides and bulletin boards.
Printed copies also available: for details see 'References and further reading'.)

JANET addresses of 74 online public access library catalogue services (OPACS), with notes on access to JANET from the Internet, the European research networks attached to IXI, and the international public packet-switched networks.

Aberdeen University
Aston University
Bath University
Bradford University
Birmingham University
Bristol University
Brunel University
Cambridge University
City of London Polytechnic
City University
Cranfield Institute of Technology
Dundee College of Technology
Dundee University
Durham University
East Anglia University
Edinburgh University
Essex University
Exeter University
Glasgow University
Hatfield Polytechnic
Heriot-Watt University
Hull University
Kent University
Lancaster University
Leeds Polytechnic
Leeds University
Leicester Polytechnic
Leicester University
Liverpool University
London University
  : Central Libertas Consortium
  : BLPES (LSE)
  : Imperial
  : Kings
  : QMW
  : RHBNC
  : UCL
  : Union List of Serials

Loughborough University
Manchester University
National Library of Wales
Newcastle University
NISSPAC
Nottingham University
Open University
Oxford Polytechnic
Oxford University
Polytechnic of Central London
Polytechnic South West
Queens University Belfast
Reading University
Royal Greenwich Observatory
Rutherford Appleton Laboratory
Salford University
Sheffield University
South Bank Polytechnic
Southampton University
St Andrews University
Staffordshire Polytechnic
Stirling University
Strathclyde University
Surrey University
Sussex University
Thames Polytechnic
Trinity College Dublin
Ulster University
UMIST, Manchester
University of Wales Libraries:
  St David's University College
  University College of North Wales, Bangor
  University College of Swansea
  University College of Wales, Aberystwyth
  University of Wales College of Cardiff
  University of Wales College of Medicine
Warwick University
York University

Figure 15. Over 70 OPACs are now accessible across JANET.

plemented in other departments of artificial intelligence and cognitive science. The software used to support *CLBib@cogs.sussex.ac.uk* (a bibliography on computational linguistics) returns a tagged bibliography in the UNIX "roffbib" format to e-mail messages sent with a subject line of simple commands (for example, for general information, Subject: Help) or lists of keywords to be searched in combination.

Online Searching of Commercial Hosts

The major benefit to libraries, in terms of cost and convenience, of their connection to the network, has probably been in its use as a route to the major online hosts: DIALOG, Datastar, Orbit, Lexis, etc. JANET has gateways linking it to British Telecom's PSS/GDN network. Since use of the PSS network is charged by volume of data transferred, accounts to use the gateway service are needed, but users benefit by sharing costs at the lowest corporate rate. The service is reliable, efficient, and easy to use, since mnemonic names are provided for each online host.

Nonetheless, international calls have always been expensive on public networks. The introduction of the IXI network, and the agreement of national PTTs that it could be used for services associated with academic research, has enabled the connection of major European commercial databases, for example, STN (providing Chemical Abstracts, INSPEC, etc.) and Datastar. In addition, the online information services of the European Community, for example, ECHO, are also connected. At the time of this writing, it was reported that DIALOG would shortly be providing a European service, via the Internet or NSFnet-relay.

The Bibliographic Utilities and Catalog Record Supply

Libraries acquire their catalog records in the UK from a variety of sources: there is no predominant supplier. The major service making use of JANET is the CURL service based at Manchester. The seven members of CURL, the Consortium of University Research Libraries, have each contributed its own full database to the host. To these have been added the combined BNB MARC files and the Library of Congress' "Books All" service, soon to be followed by access to OCLC. In this way, there may be multiple copies of any one record, perhaps with minor variations for the same title. Since it was established with a grant from the University Grants Committee, all academic libraries are eligible to use the service. Records can be transferred by capture off-screen (downloading) or by file transfer of batches of records using the Coloured Book NIFTP standard. Contact Curlsys@cms.umrcc.ac.uk.

SLS, the suppliers of the "Libertas" library system, developed the software for look-up and retrieval of catalog records between their systems, and use interactive communications across JANET for this purpose. Catalogers using Libertas can also retrieve records from the record supply service of OCLC. OCLC is itself connected to JANET to enable access across IXI to the large number of private research networks and public data networks in Europe.

The British Library provides access to their BLAISE services to JANET users, at normal commercial rates. These can be used online or for record selection and delivery via magnetic tape. The British Library has not sought to exploit the potential of its network connection. Contact R.Smith@jnt.ac.uk.

Finally, the other main UK bibliographic utility, BLCMP, with a carefully maintained database, still sustains its own network for its members, as does OCLC (though it is reported to be connecting in 1992). Users of BLCMP services do share in an e-mail discussion group based at Brunel.

Library Suppliers and Periodicals Agents

With the liberalization of the network—and the acceptance of connections to commercial users who work in collaboration with academic institutions—have come many enquiries and much interest from publishers, booksellers, and periodicals suppliers. JUGL held a seminar for suppliers at Aston in 1990. The suppliers are well aware that libraries would welcome closer integration of their systems. To date however, only Blackwells have connected directly to JANET and, as yet, only to provide login access to their periodicals database.

Library System Vendors

The success of JANET has depended in part on the insistence by the Computer Board that suppliers of general purpose computers should conform to a standard operational requirement for networking. Sadly, this obligation did not extend to library systems (in the early 1980s, classified by the then University Grants Committee as furniture!), since the Computer Board at that time had no charge to fund or approve their purchase. As a result, their suppliers, pleading cost or "lack of demand," have avoided the need to provide integrated access for library staff and users alike to electronic mail, file transfer, or to participate in OSI-based developments in interlending or catalog record access. However, the prevalence of UNIX is making itself felt even in libraries, four suppliers (CLSI, Dynix, VTLS, and Reflexion) are now marketing library systems that will run on a UNIX platform, and a new generation of interconnectable systems is in development.

The ISC now has a charge to direct library systems computing, and it is to be hoped that it will impose the same requirements for effective networking as for general purpose academic systems.

Developing the Use of Open Systems Protocols for Library Purposes

The full use of networks will depend upon the close integration at the systems level of widely distributed applications and their users. The generic example is of client-server applications where a user can communicate using common protocols through a familiar desktop interface to a variety of distant databases. The library world was early to recognize this need; the first IR (information retrieval) protocol was submitted as an American National Standard in 1983. Most recently, the potential of WAIS (wide-area information services) communicating using the Z39.50 IR protocol (related to the OSI SR—search and retrieve—standard) has created much interest.

The work in the United States and the United Kingdom on developing SR and related OSI library services (for example, ILL) has been well reviewed by Lorcan Dempsey in *Libraries, Networks and OSI*, 1991, and world-wide by Gary Cleveland in the IFLA UDT publication, *Research Networks and Libraries: Applications and Issues for a Global Information Network*, 1991. However, work in the United Kingdom is not specific to JANET and is therefore outside the scope of this review. The recent "request for tenders" for the CEC Action Plan for Libraries, part of the DG XIII Telematics program, and the change in role of the ISC discussed above, is expected to stimulate more activity.

Conclusion

JANET has become a reliable and highly valued component of British academic life. Despite a widely-shared view in the United Kingdom of the inadequacy of current funding for both higher education and scientific research, and despite major changes in the coordination of policy for university computing, the future of JANET and the beginnings of SuperJANET seem assured.

Several factors should contribute to the development of a wide and well-supported community of users over the next few years. Policy making and the formal management of the technical infrastructure, always reliable despite constant development and change, will soon be coordinated by a new and more broadly based body: UKERNA. This will manage and carry forward the work of the Joint Network Team, responsible for the operation of the JANET network, the implementation of emerging applications standards, and for advice on networking on individual campuses, and thus in a position to support the full integration of all forms of distributed working. This new body must provide the research and educational community in the UK with robust solutions to the major current problems—of concluding the protocol transition to OSI, of coexistence with TCP/IP standards, and of close integration within a European framework.

Beyond primarily technical considerations, the Network User Groups, whose participation has been an integral part of the operation since JANET was conceived, are now encouraging a greater level of publicity, training, and support. Their objectives are shared by the several nationally supported initiatives to provide more information services (bibliographic, text-based, statistical, and numeric) along the network, and to improve awareness in all disciplines of information technology, software, and other resources. Finally, since this overview is partly aimed at librarians and information providers, they are the providers of specialized library services and the national libraries, well placed to extend the efficiency of conventional services. The new professional roles that are emerging for these groups, of wide-ranging support for the academic and research activity of their users, will need to be complemented by new systems and networked resources; concepts that will prove the potential of a true open systems world. For in the end, the network will be defined by the people who use it, and by the information they gain from and contribute to it. [The opinions expressed here are the author's and in no way reflect the views of the University of Sussex or any other organization.]

References and Further Reading

(For information on publications of the Joint Network Team, apply to The Joint Network Team, Rutherford Appleton Laboratory, Chilton, Didcot, Oxon, OX11 0QX, UK—JANET-Liaison-Desk@jnt.ac.uk.)

Academic Community OSI Transition Group. 1987. *Transition to OSI Standards.* Joint Network Team.

Buckle, David. 1991. Networking Across Europe. *OCLC Newsletter.* November/December: 26-27.

Cleveland, Gary. 1991. *Research Networks and Libraries: Applications and Issues for a Global Network.* International Federation of Library Associations and Institutions. (Available from the IFLA International Office for Universal Dataflow and Telecommunications, c/o National Library of Canada.)

Computers in Teaching Initiative Support Service. *The CTISS File.* Three issues a year. (Available from: CTISS, University of Oxford, 13 Banbury Road, Oxford, OX2 6NN.)

Cooper, R., J. Hutton, and I. Smith. 1991. From JANET to SuperJANET: The Development of a High Performance Network to Support UK Higher Education and Research. *Computer Networks and ISDN Systems* 21: 347-351.

Cooper, R. 1988. The JANET Internet. *Computer Bulletin* 10: 149-153.

Dempsey, Lorcan. 1991. *Libraries, Networks and OSI*. Westport, CT: Meckler.

Foster, Jill. 1992. *Status Report on User Support and Information Services on Rare Member Networks 24/1/92*. (Available by e-mail to mailbase@newcastle.ac.uk, with the text *send RARE-WG3-USIS status.01.92*.)

Inter-University Committee on Computing. 1990. *Directory of Computer Services, 1990-91*. (Available from IUCC@Durham.ac.uk.)

IUCC/SCONUL. Joint Information Services Working Party. 1990. *Report on Information Technology Penetration and Co-ordination on University Campuses*. IUCC. (Also published as: 1990. Computer-based Information Services in Universities. *British Journal of Academic Librarianship* 5 (1): 1-30.)

JANET-LIBMAIL: Libraries on JANET, Their Staff and Services: An E-mail Directory. 1991. University of Sussex Library.

JANET-OPACS: Online Public Access Catalogues in the UK. 1991. University of Sussex Library.

Joint European Networking Conference. 1990. Proceedings. In *Computer Networks and ISDN Systems* 19 (3-5).

Joint European Networking Conference. 1991. Proceedings. In *Computer Networks and ISDN Systems* 23 (1-3).

Joint Network Team. *Network News*. Issued regularly, free.

Joint Network Team. 1991. *Proceedings*. JANET User Support Workshop, Canterbury, September 10-11, 1991.

Joint Network Team. 1990. *The JANET Starter Pack: Introductory Information About Janet*.

JUGL Newsletter: Network News and Developments for Libraries. four issues a year. (For information on subscribing to JUGL, contact: Mrs. J. Yeadon, Lyon Playfair Library, Imperial College, London, SW7 2AZ— cmaas06@vaxa.cc.ic.ac.uk.)

Project JUPITER. *Guide for Libraries on JANET.*

Project JUPITER. *The Jupiter Training Pack: For Training Library Staff in Using JANET.* (Available from The University Library, Hillhead Street, Glasgow, G12 8QE.)

Moon, Brenda. 1986. Cooperative Networks and Service to the Scholar: University Library Resources for Online Research. *British Journal of Academic Librarianship* 1: 41-52.

[The Nelson Report] *Report of a Working Party on Computer Facilities for Teaching in Universities.* 1983. Computer Board for Universities and Research Councils.

Stone, Peter. 1991. *JANET: A Report on Its Use for Libraries.* British Library (Research Paper 77). (Available from BL Document Supply Center, Boston Spa, LS23 7BQ.)

Thomas, David. 1991. Beyond the PAD. *UC&R Newsletter* 33 (Spring): 6-13.

High-Tech Information Network in High Energy Physics

Ann-Sofi Israelson, Achille Petrilli, Mogens Sandfaer, and Stephan Schwarz
CERN (European Organization for Nuclear Research)
Geneva, Switzerland

Abstract

High Energy Physics is a research area where extreme demands are set on timely and comprehensive access to bibliographic and full-text information. The normal distribution channels, i.e. major commercial databases and journal publishing, are not satisfactory: the main literature is manuscripts (preprints) hitherto circulated en masse, and internationally accessible databases are updated daily. This chapter describes recent high-tech applications of electronic storage and networking and of the organizational and systems design problems that are to be dealt with on a world-wide scale.

Preamble: The Global Village

In times of fast development, actors in the center of events have a distinctive advantage. Effective participation requires current knowledge of what is going on ("the right information in the right form at the right time"). The idea of a "global village," when introduced in the sociology of communication some decades back, expresses the confidence in modern communications and computing technology to overcome the obstacle of distance and time delays. This, as we all know, is an oversimplification: the complexities of human communication cannot be reduced to signals and processes in cables and computers. Yet, there are areas, for example, in well-defined scientific areas with coherent research communities and a *lingua franca*, where access to, and dissemination of current information makes global participation possible. It is in this sense that recent developments in information services in High Energy Physics (HEP) make the label "global village" justified by covering the entire research community, including groups in the Third World. The solutions found may prove to be relevant to many other areas as a pilot study.

The HEP Community

The area of High Energy Physics (or Particle Physics) is concerned with the study of the fundamental properties of the physical world: how and why things are the way they are, right back to the origin of the universe. To achieve experimental conditions revealing such properties, one has to build particle accelerators of ever greater energies. This requires cooperation between physicists and technicians in a wide range of high-tech areas, including materials, vacuum, superconductivity, electronics, and computers. In fact, recent advances in accelerator and detector technology have contributed a great deal to these areas. A brief but very informative and readable historical account is given in *The Hunting of the Quark* by Michael Riordan.[1]

A current directory[2] lists about 1,000 HEP institutes and laboratories from 70 countries, but only a few of these have their own accelerators. In most cases, experimental physicists participate in huge international collaborations, related to experiments at the major accelerator laboratories. One of these is CERN, the European Laboratory for Particle Physics near Geneva on the border between Switzerland and France. CERN has an annual budget of about $9 million, over 3,000 employees, 5,000 associates not on CERN payroll, and over 200 universities/institutions participating in its projects. Another is SLAC (Stanford Linear Accelerator Center), at present our principal United States counterpart in information services.

Timeliness, Grey Literature, and the "Preprints Culture"

Scientific communication has always had an important element of informal communication. The real progress happens within "invisible colleges" in the sense of Derek Price[3] by direct contacts, letters, and transmission of manuscripts (now even by fax, FTP, or e-mail) long before publishing. However, this process can work only on a limited scale, providing access by privilege. In any dynamic science, the time factor is of prime importance for *all* participants, and may call for new ways to disseminate information, when the delays of the traditional publishing system are unacceptable. The advent of electronic journals is a case in point for sophisticated solutions, but it requires technical coordination and compatibility of input and advanced equipment for access. A more conventional but highly effective method (although with obvious financial implications) is the production of *local print runs* for direct distribution to colleagues and institutions.

Curiously, it is through the dependence of the HEP community on the rapid and reliable distribution of this kind of "clandestine publishing" (a typical case of grey literature, normally not manageable by libraries), that a service could be designed and established, meeting the rather extreme information requirement of the community. To explain this peculiarity and its implications, a few remarks on the concept of grey literature are needed.

The term "grey literature" covers a wide range of quasi-publications, with one feature in common; they are not really public, i.e. easily accessible on the publishing market or in libraries other than highly specialized collections. There are different reasons for avoiding the regular publishing market: cost, commercial interest, confidentiality, a limited audience, and the speed of dissemination. New techniques for storage, access, and reproduction have precipitated the erosion of any demarcation lines: the shades of grey multiply, and what appears grey to some, may be ivory or pure white to others.

A particular feature of communications in HEP is the dominance of the "preprints culture." The preprint, i.e. the manuscript ready to be submitted to conferences or journals, is by far the most important source for information transfer on the research front in HEP, to the extent that there has developed a veritable "preprints culture" with its own social structure. Transgressing the concept of an "invisible college," the shortcutting of the lengthy publishing process involves the entire community. The preprint has become the main medium for communicating recent results. Therefore, the flow of preprints has become highly organized, to the point of "whitewashing the grey literature" so that it effectively becomes public/published the day it leaves the author's desk.

The flow of preprints in the HEP community in the majority of cases compares quantitatively with the distribution of specialized journals. A print run of 1,000 copies is not unusual. About 12,000 preprints are issued annually, and most of them end up as published articles in journals or proceedings of conferences. However, direct mailing to institutions and individuals, and the additional self-service photocopying in a few places where there are comprehensive collections (approaching one million pages a year in the CERN library), obviously does not grant access to all concerned. Scientists in smaller HEP-environments, the home institutions of most HEP-scientists—whether they participate in experiments in the main labs or not—normally would not have access to all this material. They would be on a number of mailing lists, and for the rest they would have to write to the authors to receive specified preprints.

A necessary condition for awareness of recent material and for orientation in the full literature of the area is the existence of an informative database, fully up-to-date, and easily accessible to the community, effectively backed up by full-text document delivery service.

Information Services to the International HEP Community

Figure 1 shows the structure of the information services in HEP, as set up at CERN (where some elements are in the implementation stage or in various developmental stages). The discussion brings to evidence how the extreme requirements on timeliness and comprehensiveness affect the routines and the international cooperation needed to make the service work as a world-wide facility.

The Database Production System

The PREP (preprints) database is the backbone of information services in HEP. The international effort dates back to the 1960s, and the most complete database now counts about 200,000 records.

The difficulties of producing a database answering the needs expressed by the users are evident from the following list:

- The records should be very comprehensive, including, *inter alia*: all authors with affiliations, title of paper, report number, locus of expected publication, keywords added from controlled vocabulary, added free subject terms, and citations.

- The titles often contain character strings or formulae containing non-latin characters and sub/superscripts. In many cases, such strings have to be made searchable for a normal keyboard, as well as displayed intelligibly on screen and printed correctly (see Figure 2).

- The big experimental collaborations in this archetypal "Big Science," result in author lists of up to 500 authors from as many as 50 institutions.

- Once the preprint has been published, the PREP record has to be updated with the reference to the relevant journal or proceedings volume.

- The users require immediate access to the information, both for searching in the database and for full-text documents.

The main problem is timing. Users in the main centers want the database to be updated within a day or two of arrival of the preprint, and the document available on display at the same time. This requirement of currency has made it difficult to avoid a considerable overlap of work: the same preprints are processed in several HEP centers simultaneously, to produce essentially the same records. Considerable multiple effort could be avoided—and the time delays of entry even shortened—if uniform routines could be established allowing decentralized input and online procedures to handle the exchange and merging of catalog records. This, however, requires a high degree of agree-

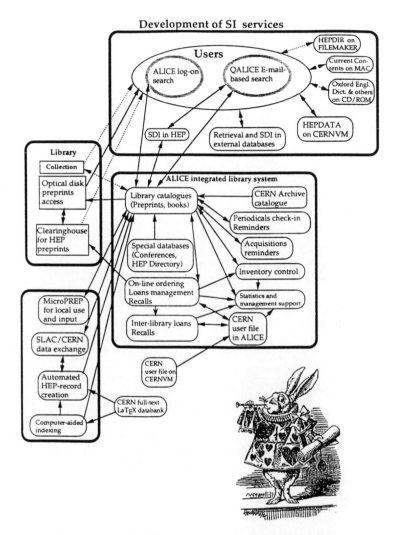

Figure 1. The structure of information services in HEP at CERN.

ment on input conventions and standards, compatibility of data, and control of data flow. Perhaps foremost, it requires compromises on both software, cataloging, and timing "philosophy," which, with an adequate metaphor might be called "strong interaction," rather than the present "weak interaction" (these are metaphors taken from the HEP vocabulary). For example, insistence from one center that a 24-hour cycle for input is indispensable (there are always users who would affirm their need of this service, particularly if it

88-0366　　Checchia, P
NA27 Collaboration
　　Lifetime of the charmed particles $D^{\pm}$, D^0, Λ_c [NA27
experiment]
Hadrons, quarks and gluons: Proceedings, 22nd Rencontre
de Moriond - Hadrons, quarks and gluons, Les Arcs, 15 -
21 Mar 1987 / Ed. by J Tran Thanh Van. - Gif-sur-Yvette :
Ed. Frontières, 1987. - (M54). - 211-217

88-0616　　Kernel, G; Korbar, D; Križan, P; Mikuž, M;
Sever, F; Stanovnik, A; Zavrtanik, D; Van Eijk, C W E;
Lourens, W; Clark, A S; Michaelis, E G; Tanner, N W
　　Measurement of the reaction $\pi^- p \to \pi^- \pi^+ n$ near
threshold [SC77 experiment]
Medium energy physics : Proceedings, International
symposium on medium-energy physics, Beijing, 23 - 28 Jun
1987 / Ed. by Chiang Huangching and Zheng Linsheng. -
Singapore : World Sci., 1987. - 604-605

88-0636　　Kwan, S
ACCMOR Collaboration
　　Λ_c and $\bar{\Lambda}_c$ production in 230 GeV π^- Cu interactions
[NA32 experiment]
Proceedings, v 1, International Europhysics conference on
high energy physics, Uppsala, 25 Jun - 1 Jul 1987 / Ed. by
O Botner. - Uppsala : Univ., 1987. - 214-215

88-0735　　Palano, A
　　Results on 0^{-+}, 1^{++} resonances and glueball
candidates [WA76 experiment] [CERN PRE 87-103]
Hadrons, quarks and gluons, proceedings, 22nd Rencontre
de Moriond - Hadrons, quarks and gluons, Les Arcs, 15 -
21 Mar 1987 / Ed. by J Tran Thanh Van. - Gif-sur-Yvette :
Ed. Frontières, 1987. - (M54). - 649-664

Figure 2. Examples of "funny characters" in HEP at CERN.

is offered free of charge), makes decentralized input practically impossible. Note, however, that there is no requirement to use the same database management software, as long as an agreed exchange format can be generated.

Automated Catalog Record Creation. Actually, a bibliographic record could in principle be created largely from the output file of the author's text processing system, given that certain standards were adhered to at the input stage (for current work on appropriate standards[4,5]). Preferred text processing systems for preprints production in HEP are LaT$_E$X (for text with formulae) and MS-WORD, which could be regarded as quasi-standards. The text-processed file is translated into SGML, using the Document Type Definition (DTD) from the American Association of Publishers.[6] The conversion is made by means of the software package XTRAN(r) (from Exoterica Inc.).

The principles of a system for automated creation of a bibliographic record from the full-text document is shown in Figure 3. A preprint full-text file is retrieved from the electronic SGML document store (author=Khoze). The elements needed for the bibliographic record are extracted and converted to ALICE format, with additional character translation to DEC standards. Eventual conversion problems are logged for study and amendment of translation tables. The corrected final version (with abstract) is entered into the bibliographic file.

At this stage, the data elements are readily identifiable by the system. The bibliographically relevant data are thus extracted, reformatted according to the cataloging rules, and combined to form a new record. The abstract can, of course, be added. Since the same electronic text source is used by publishers like AIP or Elsevier, the reference to the published article (so-called anti-preprint data) could be downloaded from the publisher as soon as it has been decided in the journal editing process, and merged into the original preprints record, i.e. long before the corresponding issue appears in print.

This project is not yet at the operational stage. Actually, the problem is still to obtain text files with standardized mark-up from the authors. The second process, creating the bibliographic record from the converted SGML file, is ready for production runs.

An interesting project still remote from the production stage, aims at computer-aided indexing from the computer-readable full-text document. It is pursued in cooperation with the University of Darmstadt. Basically, the AIR/X system, applied in producing the Physics Briefs database in FIZ/Karlsruhe, is used for linguistic analysis on the special language of HEP in an effort to extract relevant keywords and relate them to their correct synonyms in a bound vocabulary.[7]

The Cooperation Potential. The present flow of bibliographic records or update information is shown in Figure 4. It is clear that the SLAC (the Stanford Linear Accelerator) information service plays a key role. The SPIRES system used by SLAC is implemented in KEK (Japan) and DESY (Germany) to

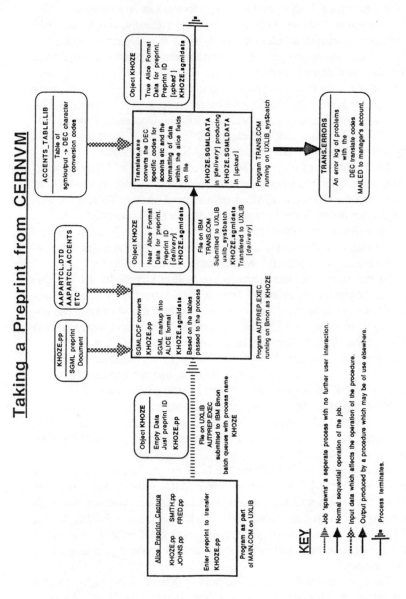

Figure 3. The process of creating a bibliographic record from the full-text document.

facilitate local operations and daily data transfer. Figure 5 emphasizes the tripartite cooperation between SLAC, DESY, and CERN, and the development of a system for distributed responsibility, using appropriate systems for data transmission, identification, and merging. Actually, as the introduction of a clearinghouse for full-text document delivery emerges, the need for local document stores is reduced. National production in HEP could be handled by national focal points, as in INIS but with the HEP timeliness requirements, and transmitted electronically to the regional focal points, as is already done in the SLAC-KEK (Tokyo) relationship and will be tested in CERN-Moscow and CERN-Beijing cooperations.

SLAC/CERN Exchange. An outline of a system under development at CERN for automated data exchange is presented in Figure 6. In principle, a document identification key is created from bibliographic data elements in the record (somewhat along the lines of the "Universal Standard Bibliographic Code" investigated in the context of the EEC DOCDEL project for published articles).[8] For grey literature, the unique identification is more difficult since the unique publication data are missing, and since the input conventions differ. This is taken care of by a sequence of nested comparisons, sorting the genuine matches from spurious ones, and finding genuinely new records.[9] The coordination problems will be clarified in the testing process and subsequently solved by agreements. Once the record is tagged by a unique identifier, future update operations can be done automatically from records received.

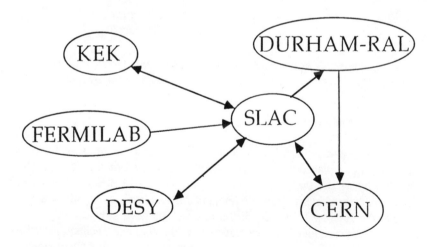

Figure 4. Present flow of records in cooperation on HEP database production.

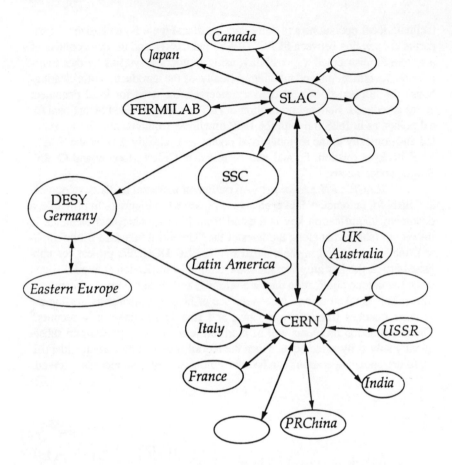

Figure 5. A possible future model for decentralized input to HEP database, meeting the requirements of coverage, timelines, and comprehensiveness.

The Database Management System

In 1990 the previous CDS/ISIS system, used for management of the library's database, was replaced by ALICE (ALEPH Library Information for CERN). This is why we use the Tenniel rabbit as a logo.[10] ALEPH(r) is an international and commercially available integrated library system, originally developed at the Hebrew University in Jerusalem. The new, radically improved, version 3 was developed in cooperation with the National Technological Library (DTB) in Copenhagen.[11] In the course of the implementation at CERN, a number of further enhancements have been introduced.

SLAC → CERN Transfer System.
System Description

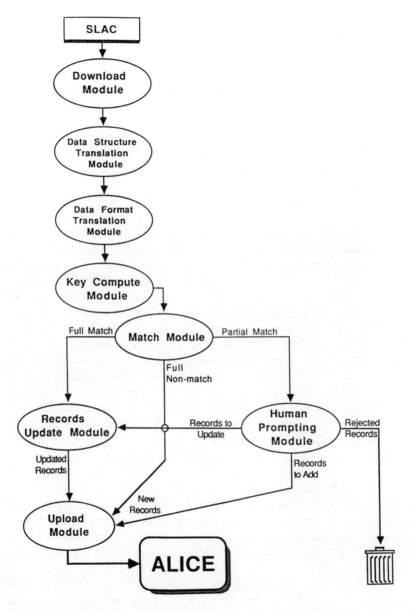

Figure 6. Outline of a system for semi-automated database updating and merging from imported records.

The main strength of the system, which runs on DEC equipment, and is now also available in UNIX versions, is its flexible tool-box approach to functional extension, its adherence to standards, and its orientation towards networking and the needs of remote users. Examples of standards implemented are ISO 8777 (common command language), ISO 8859 (character set), ISO 2709 (data export), and PostScript output for printing. Among special features added are the handling of very large bibliographic records, special links between main records and sub-records (for example, proceedings and contributed papers), an e-mail retrieval facility with an SDI (Selective Dissemination of Information) option, a link to full-text storage devices and special retrieval modes for document archive catalogs. Some of these developments have been made as the result of direct systems development cooperation between ALEPH and CERN.

The User Access Channels

In order to make the systems and resources of the Scientific Information Service available to campus and world-wide users, special attention has been given to access channels compatible with the normal computer environment at CERN (IBM/VM and VAX/VMS systems, as well as various UNIX systems).

Access Diagram. The different combinations of local equipment and modes of networking to be operated to gain access to the library computer are shown in Figure 7. There remain some gateway insufficiencies between the IBM and DEC systems, which turn up as limitations on the user interface. In the majority of cases, however, users have alternatives which are fully satisfactory. Recently, the system has become available world-wide on Internet.

The QALICE system with SDI function: The elements of a sophisticated device created at CERN by Lian Yachun, a computer scientist from IS-TIC, Beijing, are shown in the flow diagram, Figure 8. It is inspired by design ideas of QSPIRES (developed at SLAC for a VM environment), providing access to database retrieval without normal password-controlled logon to the platform. The design for a VAX environment turned out to meet with unexpected difficulties, to which elegant solutions were found. Essentially, access is gained by using a Message or Tell command, or by an e-mail message sent to the computer. This message contains a single or a chain of search strings, which are picked up and sent to the retrieval system. The retrieval is then carried out, and the resulting file is sent to the requestor's local e-mail account.[12]

This system therefore makes it possible for anyone on any network reaching out to CERN, to access the library files and carry out searches. The system is enhanced with a module for SDI services to the international community. Presently, about 300 profiles are on the PREP preprints database.

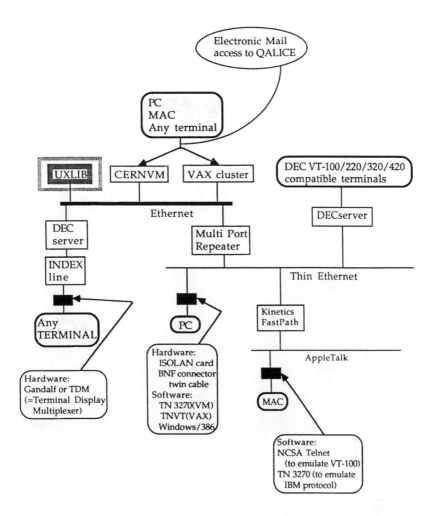

Figure 7. Access to the ALICE library system and document server at CERN.

Another effort to facilitate the exploitation of CERN preprint records is the MicroPREP database management system, an application of the flexible MicroISIS system from UNESCO, running on IBM-compatible personal computers.[13] It is geared to operate on a subfile of the CERN PREP file, which is currently updated either via data transfer or from disks received by mail. Since the software is in the open domain, this is an ideal product for installation in LDCs (Less Developed Countries) and in other remote institutes without easy online access to CERN. Until now, for document delivery

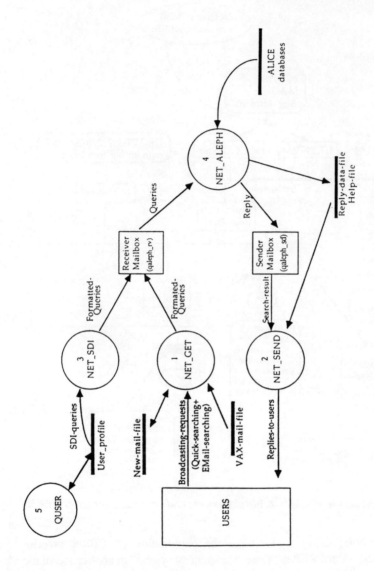

Figure 8. Data flow diagram of the QALICE system (level 0).

the requestor had to contact the originator of the preprint. The creation of an international clearinghouse will change this situation.

The Directory of HEP Institutes. This is a file on ALICE, providing comprehensive up-to-date information on HEP institutes throughout the world: name and address, all telecommunications addresses/codes, short descriptions of research programs and accelerators. It is currently updated from information received. A Filemaker-Pro(r) version for Macintoshes has been designed and is available on disk or via file server, for local installation and operation of the file for retrieval, address label printing, etc. There is also a printed version.

The Library, with Automated Document Access and Clearinghouse

The CERN library was created as a modest institutional library in the mid-1950s. It has specialized in particle physics, with areas related to accelerator and detector construction. The collection consists of about 40,000 volumes (weeded regularly to provide space), about 1,000 current periodicals, and over 120,000 preprints and reports. One main problem is the inconsistent requirement of open access 24 hours every day, and staffing; at a maximum of 40 hours a week. The "loss" rate is astounding, particularly for recent material, including recent preprints (an average of 15 percent of the current week's display disappears, mainly items in high demand). The use of the collections is illustrated by the production of self-service photocopies approaching one million per year.

Optical Disk Document Access System. The ideal solution to this problem is furnished by the optical disc (WORM) storage technique. The obsolescence of preprints is a fast process, in most cases less than a year (the lead time for journal publishing). With standard compression techniques, the storage capacity needed for one year's preprints is on the order of 12-15GB (gigabytes). This means a couple of 12-inch disk stations for 6.4GB disks, or the equivalent amount in a jukebox. New preprints should be scanned within a day of arrival, and logically linked to the corresponding bibliographic record in ALICE. The DORODOC(r) system from the French firm DoroTech (related to Thomson-France), using French, U.S. and Japanese products is now installed at CERN to create an application called DARS (Document Archiving and Retrieval System.)[14] The setup shown in Figure 9, with software, scanner printer, two powerful workstations, and about 17GB of optical storage accessible via a jukebox, can be obtained for $160,000. The ALICE <<—>> DARS <<—>> USER-workstation interactions for document image access are shown in Figure 10. The description of events, referring to the numbers on the figure, is as follows:

1. The user initiates a session on ALICE from his/her workstation, via TELNET from UNIX, Mac, and PC, or via set host from VMS. From here all ALICE possibilities are available.

2. Upon request from the user to display a preprint, a connection to the viewer server residing on DARS is established. The preprint ID and the user specified workstation name are sent via this connection to the DARS.

3. The viewer server validates the workstation name and then activates a viewing process on the user workstation. At this point the DARS disconnects from ALICE and leaves the user in charge of the viewing window.

A typical retrieval and display sequence is shown in Figures 11-14. A bibliographic record is found, the scanned image is requested and displayed. The present access time on campus for the first page of a preprint is about 15 seconds for retrieval, decompression, and transmission. A central automatic printing facility will generate hardcopies equivalent to the original, to be picked up by the requestor. Central printing can be ordered online by any remote user of the ALICE system. There will be an option for automated fax transfer. With Group-3 technique, some loss of resolution is inevitable, but with broadband networks in preparation, Group-4 technology will provide high-speed document delivery of quality equivalent to the original. This document delivery system is in line with current projects in France.[15] It is also possible to modify the QALICE system to allow for printing commands to be sent. With the Internet and e-mail modes of access to the database, and the image server facilities, an international clearinghouse for preprints is established.

The Global Village Revisited

It is seen that the various components of the "grand scheme" jointly form a pattern of information resources management (IRM) and service production that reaches out world-wide, with minimal delays even for remote users in poor institutions: the distributed network of regional PREP data input centers (foreseen in the design), the controlled data flow for a common comprehensive database in several main laboratories, the various modes of database access, and the international clearinghouse for preprints.

By having access, timely and comprehensively, to new information, the disadvantage of distance experienced by HEP physicists all over the world will be reduced, sometimes dramatically. This is particularly, but not

Preprint storage and retrieval

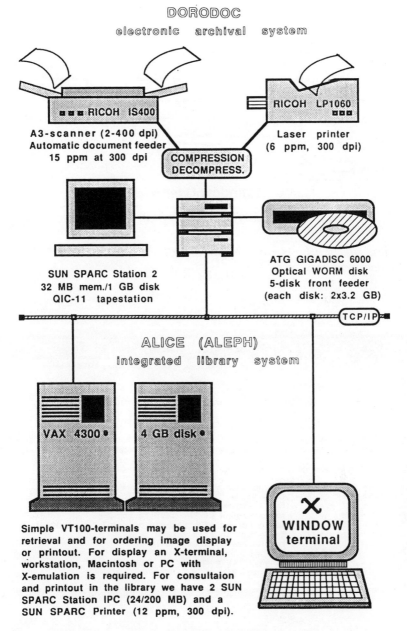

Figure 9. CERN full-text document access setup (image server connected to library).

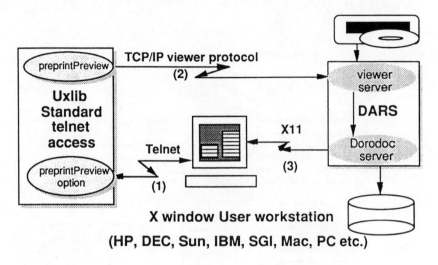

Figure 10. ALICE <<—>> DARS <<—>> USER-workstation interactions for document image access.

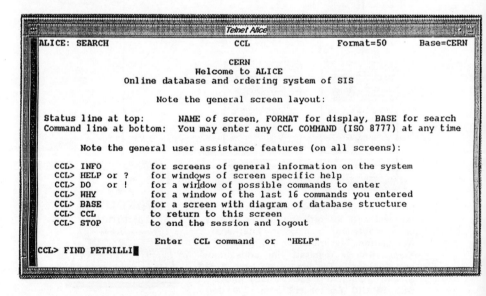

Figure 11. Example of command sequence to retrieve and display a document.

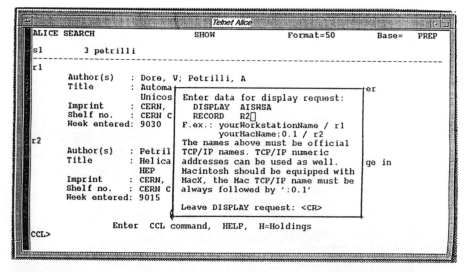

Figure 12 .

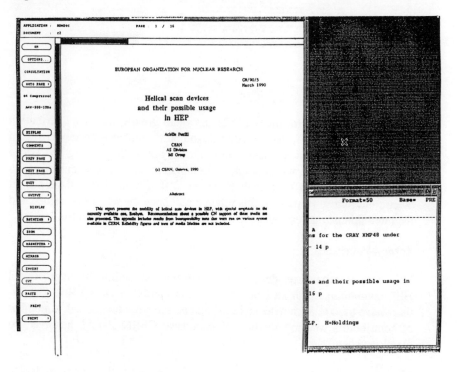

Figure 13.

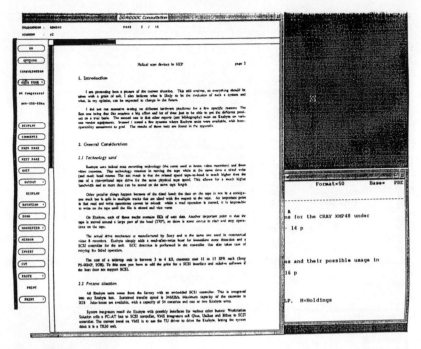

Figure 14.

exclusively, the case for many LDCs and small groups. Massive distribution of preprints can be effectively reduced, and partly replaced by services from the clearinghouse, which reaches out to groups not on the mailing lists (since in HEP as elsewhere, the principle of cumulative advantage is operating, so that "unto those who have shall be given").[16] The Global Village has an electronic library. Hopefully, this scheme will have the resources needed and the international interest and cooperation necessary to bring it to fruition.

Acknowledgements

This chapter reports on developments carried out within the international HEP community, with an emphasis on contributions from CERN. The authors have tried to acknowledge in the text all the work mentioned. A number of contributors working for limited periods at CERN should, however, be mentioned here:

Mr. Lian Yachun from ISTIC, Beijing (QALICE with SDI, and MicroPREP); Ms. K. Renfrew and Mr. G. Mead from the University of Manchester (automated indexing project), Mr. F. Falcoz, from Webster University (data exchange and ALICE systems implementation), and Mr. B. Oxnard from Staffordshire Polytechnic (automated record creation). The cooperation with the MI (Management Information) Group and CN (Computers and Networks) Division at CERN and the contributions of Ms. M. Gracco and Mr. W. Simon (current work on system and production) are key ingredients in the eventual success. The Master Brain of the ALICE system is Mr. Y. Spruch (Aleph Yissum, Jerusalem). The cooperative attitude of the systems vendor, Ex Libris Inc., Tel Aviv, to unconventional requirements is appreciated.

References

1. Riordan, M. 1987. *The Hunting of the Quark.* New York: Simon & Schuster.

2. *Directory of Research Institutes in High Energy Physics.* 1992. Geneva: CERN. (Database on the ALICE system at CERN, also available as a FilemakerPro database for Macintosh.)

3. de Solla Price, D. J. 1986. *Little Science, Big Science . . . and Beyond.* Columbia University Press.

4. Goosens, M. and E. van Herwijnen. 1991. *Scientific Text Processing.* CERN AS-MI/91-02.

5. Goosens, M. and E. van Herwijnen. 1991. *The Elementary Particle Notation (PEN) Scheme.* CERN AS-MI/91-04.

6. Oxnard, B. 1987. *Automatic CERN Preprint Upload.* Draft project report, CERN (AS-SI)—*Standard for Electronic Manuscript Preparation and Markup.* Washington, DC: Association of American Publishers, 1987.

7. Biebricher, P., et al. 1988. The Automatic Indexing System AIR/PHYS—From Research to Application. *Proceedings of the 1988 ACM Conference on R&D in Information Retrieval*, editor, Y. Chiaramella. Presses Universitaires de Grenoble.—Renfrew, K. 1991. *Research on Automatic Indexing System AIR/X with Respect to a High Energy Physics Database.* Draft report, CERN (AS-SI).

8. Falcoz, F. 1991. *Automated Comparison and Merging of Bibliographic Records.* Draft project report, CERN (AS-SI).

9. Ayres, F.H. 1987. *Electronic Document Delivery—The Linkage Between Bibliographic and Full-text Databases.* CEC Report EUR 10677 EN, Luxembourg.

10. Carroll, L. *Alice in Wonderland.* (Ill. by Sir John Tenniel.)

11. Sandfaer, M. 1991. Remote Access—The True Test of the OPAC as a Front-end of Library Services. *Proceedings of the Third Anglo-Nordic Seminar on OPACs and the User,* 69-89. Cranfield Conference Center April 8-11, 1990, British Library R&D Report 6040.

12. Yachun, Lian. 1990. *QALICE Design Description.* CERN (AS-SI) 90-01.— *QALICE User's Guide.* CERN (AS-SI) 90-02.—*QALICE Manager Guide.* CERN (AS-SI) 90-03.—*QALICE Programs.* CERN (AS-SI) 90-04.

13. Yachun, Lian. 1989. *Introduction to the MicroPREP Data Base System.* CERN (TH-SIS) 89-02.—*MicroPREP File Preparation.* CERN (AS-SI) 90-05, 1990.

14. Petrilli, A. 1991. *Automatic Preprint Handling—Technical Specification.* Draft Report. CERN (AS-MI), January 22, 1991.—*Integrating a Document Archiving and Retrieval Facility with the ALICE Library System.* CERN (AS-MI) report 1992, in preparation.

15. Fabreguettes, C. 1989. Le Projet Foudre. *Documentaliste* 26: 239-247, and the CNRS Project. *Système d'archivage Numérique.*

16. Merton, R. K. 1988. The Matthew Effect in Science (part II): Cumulative Advantage and the Symbolism of Intellectual Property. *ISIS* 79: 606-623.

Wide-Area Network Applications for Libraries in Slovenia

Primoz Juznic and Emil Hudomalj
University of Ljubljana, Slovenia

Abstract

Wide-area networks are slowly growing in sophistication and use in Eastern Europe. Librarians in Slovenia are increasingly using WAN technology for access to bibliographic utilities and specialized information systems, and to share e-mail and undertake in cooperative collection development projects. Improvements in the information infrastructure are needed, and centralized vs. decentralized network administration models are being debated. [This case study must be read with an understanding that the events it describes have taken place against the backdrop of the recent civil war in Yugoslavia, which has caused so much suffering. In this context, the authors' efforts to carry on their pursuit of an improved networking environment and enhanced information services must be considered heroic. - Eds.]

WAN History and Administration in Slovenia

To better understand the administration and use of wide-area network applications for libraries in Slovenia, it is necessary to know something of the general history of WAN use in libraries.

The factors that have motivated the development of wide-area network (WAN) access to a variety of computing facilities offered or available to researchers all over the world have also motivated the development of WANs in Slovenia. Although this development was fragmented and uncoordinated at the beginning, many institutions have realized that a unified approach to networking is required to provide nation-wide computer communications and improved access to computer resources.

These characteristics do not differ from the development of WANs in other countries. The details of how the WAN is being developed can, of course, vary widely, but in general the goal is the same. As the diversity and sophistication of computational machinery have increased, so has the demand for networks to transport the generated information and knowledge.[1] The proliferation of computers, modems, and communications software among the general population will increase the demand for services once available

111

only to users of large computer facilities. This will in turn cause expanded use of WANs.

It is reasonable to expect that in the near future nearly every personal computer will have a modem or will be connected to networks as another way to access online services. These online services include new ways of data dissemination and scientific publication involving sophisticated database searches and electronic journals, and provide access to the public X.25 network and to wide-area networks for research and teaching purposes.

The Development of SLON

In the academic community of Slovenia, the primary hardware platform (other than personal computers) is the Digital Equipment Corporation (DEC) VAX. In the early 1980s, the existing technology already enabled connections between VAX computers. Although there was no central organization which coordinated and directed networking itself, networks nevertheless started to grow rapidly. Later, the same networks started to encompass nonacademic organizations such as industry, banks, and tourism. Today, the network consists of several hundred computers, but there is still no central administration. The network is informally called SLON (Slovenian for elephant).

Effective administration dictates that there are some points which have to be arranged among all the members of the network. Beside intensive personal contacts among system managers, there are also informal meetings once or twice a year where important topics are discussed. Technically speaking, the whole network is based on experts who each maintain a specific part. They provide an administrative base used to coordinate applications such as electronic mail, conferences, remote login, and file transfer.

The need for security, availability, and reliability of network services prompted some organizations to take care of some parts of the network or to build their own networks, and then connect them with SLON. SLON actually consists of several subnetworks that can operate independently of others.

Libraries started to use networking intensively after establishing the program Yugoslav Scientific and Technological Information System (YSTIS), discussed in detail below. Library activities have dramatically influenced the evolution of the whole Slovenian computer network.

Administering the Network

The fact that no central organization existed which could run the network was probably beneficial in the past, as it allowed free access and growth. But in the 1980s the need for availability, reliability, and speed of the whole network and its services became more pressing. The need for at least some formal administration has become apparent. And, it will be necessary to continue to improve user support, seminars, printed documents, and enhance services such as gateways to other networks and fax.

Many advances in networking have been made by the Institute Jozef Stefan in Ljubljana, which also plays a major role in establishing international links. As a result of its work in the project EUREKA/COSINE, the Yugoslav Network for Academic Community (YUNAC) was founded, which is a member of RARE (Réseaux Associés pour la Recherche Européenne). Its main activity is to represent our academic community in foreign organizations and to provide services such as electronic mail. For well-known political reasons, there arose a need to establish a similar Slovenian network organization. Some efforts have already been made toward this.

Computer Hardware and Software

The majority of computers in SLON are Digital VAXes (from microVAXes through series 4000, 6000, to 8000). Some are tied together as clusters. Almost all computers in the network utilize DECnet, the software and hardware used to connect Digital computers. From the user's point of view, it enables all computers to be equal, no matter how big they are. This and the fact that almost all computers run the VMS operating system is of great help for users who work on different computers. All libraries in Slovenia use the same equipment.

Physical connections are maintained through a packet-switching data network called JUPAK (X.25), leased lines and coaxial cables (for small distances). The number of UNIX machines in the network is small but is increasing, as is use of the TCP/IP protocol suite. Personal computer users typically access the network through dial-up lines, while some utilize PathWorks, which enables PCs to act as a node in a network.

The fact that the X.25 network in our country is connected to similar networks in other countries makes it possible to access information on an international scale. Beside X.29 connections for accessing remote computers, X.25 is used also for electronic mail (via EAN software that utilizes the X.400 protocol). Through gateways it is possible to reach all well-known international networks, such as the Internet and BITNET. Some months ago, YUNAC also started to use IXI (International X.25 Infrastructure) as an outgrowth of the COSINE project. In the near future it will be possible to apply IXI for remote login and other services.

Design and Implementation of the WAN

In the 1980s, SLON growth accelerated. Although there was no central planning, there are rules that circulate among system managers and users—some of which are disseminated via electronic conferences.

In the early stages, the allocation of addressing space was determined, and rules regarding network security and user behavior were created. More recently, efforts have been made to optimize the network topology and acquire hardware to improve performance. The network is divided into geographical or logical "areas." An area consists of computers which communicate only with each other. Some computers (designated as area routers) interconnect with other areas. Areas are defined geographically or organizationally. For example, the Slovenia network is its own area, as is Croatia. All dial-in access personal computers are grouped in a special area.

DECnet does not provide a single point where it is possible to route network traffic. It is possible to estimate total network traffic only by the services provided, users, and their applications.

Electronic mail is the basic service. Electronic conferences located on different computers are available to all users, and are perhaps the most heavily used service. These conferences cover different subjects, such as computers, networks, recreation, and discussions about specific projects. Remote login is used for accessing databases and computers with significant processing power. Other services include file transfer, remote job entry, and distributed computing.

The WAN and Libraries

Libraries and other providers of scientific information services have become one of the most important parts of the WAN in Slovenia. Online access to the central catalog is especially useful to libraries and users. Remote login to access other library catalogs and electronic mail to contact library staff are becoming increasingly important. The system of cooperative cataloging is using the WAN as its telecommunications backbone.

In Slovenia, one of the main reasons for implementing wide-area networking was to provide access to online services that would improve and modernize the existing scientific information systems. And libraries, being an important part of these systems, were the first entities to fully utilize wide-area networking as a professional tool.

Libraries Take Lead in WAN Development

Why have libraries taken this lead role? Librarians have a tradition of resource sharing and have worked together in the past in cooperative efforts (all too often doomed to failure because of the lack of proper tools). The online interactive processing capabilities of the bibliographic utilities which allow many institutions to search a database and input a record in a timely fashion and following certain guidelines and standards have made significant cooperative efforts possible.[2] The confluence of technology and the awareness of research libraries that no single library can hope to own the resources needed for modern research has encouraged computer networking in Yugoslavia.[3]

The challenge of the Yugoslav Scientific and Technological Information System was to build a nation-wide linking system made up of six partly independent systems in an uneven political system throughout Yugoslavia. During the life of the project, great differences in economic development, which clearly shape the infrastructure, became more obvious. In some parts of Yugoslavia, the first concepts or even knowledge of computer networking were introduced by libraries. The concept of a linked, nation-wide library network predicated the building of the computer network infrastructure.

Usually it is argued that networking can only be successful if it is a bottom-up, grass-roots effort; it is not and cannot be imposed from the top down. Reflecting this philosophy, Yugoslav networks were not built as centrally-managed, standardized entities, but grew through the cooperation of many institutions[4], as has been demonstrated in Slovenia.

Union Cataloging in Yugoslavia

Much has been written about "the library without walls," or the ability to access information independent of the library itself. Ten or more years ago, when we read about it, it was seen as a concept of the distant future. We read of the wonders of telecommunications networks and microcomputers enabling researchers to access all kinds of scientific information regardless of location. This vision of distributed scholarly information systems was not widely held in Slovenian libraries. Librarians were often not aware of the possibilities.

This future was suddenly imposed by the effects of the YSTIS project. Wide-area networks are usually only the tools of universities and research institutions, on an effectively free basis, or for a flat basic charge. Librarians in academic institutions began to explore the network, looking for a variety of electronic services which could fit into library operations. Libraries willing to seize the initiative saw results.

The system of union cataloging, which is the most visible and well-known wide-area networking library application, started as a federal project, part of YSTIS (with OCLC as an "idealized" example). Libraries could join since federal money was provided to procure computer hardware. The concept of union cataloging was a success. The basic conditions for the realization of such a concept were the application of information and communications technologies, which were available, the development of national and application of international standards for data processing and transfer, plus the assurance of technical support.[5]

In 1987, the Institute for Information Sciences of the University of Maribor (IZUM) was selected as a host for the Library Information System and a System of Scientific and Technical Information in Slovenia.

We have already written about the technical conditions (DECnet, X.25) for the project. The system of union cataloging allowed data to be input into a local system, automatically added to a central union catalog database (located at IZUM) with attendant security provisions, ensuring both local and network data integrity.

Yugoslav Union Catalog

Since there were more than fifty institutions in Yugoslavia actively involved in this system of shared cataloging either as full, partial, or affiliated members, the Yugoslav Union Catalog (YUBIB) could be considered as the most commendable achievement of the entire Yugoslav library community. Ironically, just as the library and information sector in Yugoslavia was finally beginning to pull together, the integrity of the whole country came under question because of the war, and Yugoslavia ceased to exist.[6] YUBIB transformed into the Cooperative Union Catalog (COBIB) and its future is uncertain. Slovenian libraries are still using it, but we are waiting to see how other libraries will react after the disintegration of Yugoslavia.

Cooperative Collection Development

An important subset of the YUBIB was the union serials catalog. This area of automation of union catalogs has altered our perception of their use. Automation has made it practical to have the lists of titles available, not only to use for information retrieval purposes, but also as a tool for the coordination of the orders among libraries in Slovenia. Thus, we have made strides toward cooperative collection development.

OPACs

Another important result of the union cataloging were online public access catalogs (OPAC). OPACs were offered through the wide-area network, and were the first application out of YUBIB-COBIB for library patrons and users. The access to the OPACs yielded another positive outcome. As libraries implemented online public access catalogs, the need for online authority control became pronounced. This need is essential, as our libraries wish to link databases and create shared catalogs. The major goal was to expand authority work procedures into the whole system to assist geographically dispersed libraries in meshing their internal authority control policies, and to provide consistent authority control state-wide.[7] This did not progress very far, so the decision was made to establish initial system-wide authority control for Slovenia alone.

Specialized Information Systems

In Slovenia the System for Scientific Information has been developed over the past 15 years. It was organized by different scientific disciplines. The System of Biomedical Information (SBMI), serving scholars and professionals, was based on principles of its close connection to biomedical science, on a coordination of libraries and information centers, their cooperation in common programs, and an orientation towards users. It was the only system which included the whole of Yugoslavia.

SBMI was organized as a decentralized and cooperative information system adjusted to the specific characteristics and needs of the country. In every republic and autonomous province, a library or an information center had been designated to coordinate all SBMI activities in that region. Representatives of these institutions were members of the Expert Committee which was responsible for the coordination of all programs and activities of the system at the federal level. Professional and technical support was offered by the Institute for Biomedical Informatics at the Medical Faculty of Ljubljana, which was designated as the Yugoslav specialized information center for biomedicine, and the coordinator of SBMI. It is formed of representatives of SBMI users in science and health care fields.[8]

Both online search and compact discs (CD-ROM) were introduced very soon after their commercial availability. Electronic conferences were also made available via computer networks. We tried to be as aggressive as possible in implementing information system accessibility through computerized wide-area networks. We found that these systems enabled researchers, regardless of their location in the country, access all kinds of automated information systems. We try to maintain these services so that they can be accessed through networks, like any other research tools. If they are valuable to our local patrons, we felt an obligation to make them widely available.[9]

The existence of SBMI gave medical libraries an important advantage as compared to libraries serving other disciplines. The system of union cataloging pushed many libraries directly into the wide-area networking world before they were prepared. Yet our Central Medical Library, as a part of the Medical Faculty, had extensive previous experience in using networks for scholarly information processes.[10]

Libraries tend to focus on databases and what they can do for them, without worrying too much about the network technologies that make database access possible. It is the ability to communicate knowledge—not to store it—that makes libraries more than warehouses. Similarly, online searching is exciting for its potential to transfer information, not for its potential to store information.[11] Library catalogs are but one special type of bibliographic database, and users of libraries search a variety of bibliographic databases.

Problems and Opportunities

Many of the problems in our application of wide-area networking in Yugoslavia were related to the political system and economic crises of the last ten years. But most of them are also problems endemic to wide-area networked library applications—the societal crises merely serve to highlight them.

Promoting Networking

Yugoslavia was never a typical East European state, and the standard of living until the mid-1970s (in Slovenia) was closer to its European neighbors—Austria and Italy—than to other East European countries. Regardless, Yugoslavia can serve as a model for how former socialist Central and Eastern Europe should respond to the challenge of networking for libraries. The economic benefits of information technology are real, and libraries can and should promote these benefits. In Slovenia, much promotion is needed. The situation is changing now; we hope that we will be a good example that networking can be implemented when a general awareness of its practical uses exists and the institutions with financial authority can be persuaded that networking is important.

Networking people tend to be both visionary and pragmatic; visionary because they have to bring to fruition the sort of future that we have seen in science fiction, and pragmatic because they still have to work with what we have today. Understanding this helps us in Slovenia to make continual incremental development steps. A major problem is getting effective telecommunications capability into Central and Eastern Europe so that other kinds of businesses will be willing to go into these regions with investments. As usual, technology is the least of the problems. Inertia and uncertainty are the real issues. In Slovenia we have found that libraries are easy to automate because they benefit from networked computing resources, but it is hard to change librarians' conservative attitudes about automation.

Two Influential Situations

Two highly influential situations have arisen. One relates to which kind of technical equipment should be used, and the other to the definition of relationships between technical services (usually called a vendor) and libraries.

The commercial X.25 network (JUPAK) has had a relatively long history in Yugoslavia; in Slovenia it started in 1986 and was fully implemented in 1988. Yet, there were clashes associated with its implementation. Although JUPAK became popular in the Republic of Slovenia, most of the six republics of the former Yugoslavia have their own technical supplier.

But as is obvious from the YSTIS project, out of which most of the library WAN applications came, there were many disparate computers to network. Yugoslavia was following the pattern set in the early 1980s in North America and Western Europe.

Academic users of computers in Eastern Europe were the first to benefit, as foreign manufacturers rushed in to fill the vacuum in the market for computers. IBM and other companies were offering their equipment to universities at little or no cost in the hope of persuading a generation of students and professors of the value of their products. The most ambitious project, so far, is the Academic Computer Initiative of IBM Europe, under which it is installing mainframe computers in Czechoslovakia, Hungary, Yugoslavia, and Poland.[12]

The failure to see substantial difference between Yugoslavia and other East European countries caused great damage to the YSTIS and the system of union cataloging. YSTIS was designed as a decentralized system, and was a compromise based on mutual interests. A "cheaper," centralized mainframe offer made the centralized-minded financing federal bodies think about other solutions to YSTIS. As a result whole systems had problems. Investments, especially in networking, dropped, and development was blocked. This is an example of how a big computer producer and poor conceptualization can actually do extensive harm. Perhaps in Yugoslavia the political tensions made such an abuse of an otherwise generous offer.

The second situation was having to choose between one vendor and one system or many different systems. The union cataloging system uses library networking. It has become obligatory and is financed by state funds. Bearing this inescapable fact in mind, libraries would be prudent to exploit the benefits received from networking into their planning process. When participants in networks are required to shift from a "local holdings" attitude to a "shared access" orientation, some autonomy is, of course, sacrificed when a library joins a network.[13]

A common vision of library networking is an environment in which libraries provide each individual in Yugoslavia an equal opportunity to access resources that will satisfy their and society's information needs and interests. However, libraries must always keep in mind that a grandiose theory has many obstacles. Libraries must contribute high-quality records. This is largely dependent on the effectiveness of the library's own technical services and the vendors from which the library acquires external technical support.

Ownership of Library Data

Equally important to a library is the safeguarding of its freedom to use the database in its own way. If the library's ownership of its machine-readable database is circumscribed by external control, then the library may be be subjected to continuous and repetitive costs in its use of data and limited in the cooperative efforts it might wish to make with other libraries or information services.

Indeed, depending on the limitations imposed, a library may find itself faced with permanent restrictions on cooperative activities with local or nation-wide libraries, not to mention other vendors and regional or national networks. There is only one rule to follow in this matter—"Protect your bibliographic data: it may be your most important investment."[14] And that advice is even more important in smaller societies where there is a danger of monopolization. Certainly no one challenged the ownership of library catalogs when they existed in paper form on cards. We feel that libraries are not sufficiently cognizant of this threat to their freedom.

Obviously, the creation of bibliographic databases is in the public interest, but granting exclusive rights to one institution can have its dangers. It can save a certain amount of money if the vendor is state subsidized, which can be the case in most smaller societies.

One problem inherent in this structure is the conflicting priorities of small and large libraries. Larger libraries typically look to their networks for a wide range of services. Smaller libraries, which do not use bibliographic utilities or search commercial or other databases, use other network services such as staff training and interlibrary loan. Any application on networks which overlooks this fact, or tries to combine both on a single compromised network, can end in the lowest possible network use.

The Mini-Network Concept

New mini-networks that consist of several carefully selected similar institutions, and have online catalogs that are accessible to each other can serve as effective alternatives, as long as they are buttressed by special interlibrary loan and document delivery systems. However, to the extent that such access tends to foster a sense of "owned" information rather than "shared" information, it becomes restrictive. A system of specialized information systems and central libraries, connecting all information centers and libraries in a certain field, and avoiding a too centralized system, can create a set of relationships that are too complex to effectively administer.

The most notable area of disagreement centers on roles that libraries, especially big ones, have in generating the national database and cooperating with other libraries to exchange records. We have also observed that the bibliographic vendor tends to see itself as also having a legitimate role in arranging such record exchanges. These problems are usually not visible when the system is being constructed.

So, by our experience, wide-area networked library applications in small countries work best by first being centralized and by concentration on one technical vendor. At a later point in its development, the system can be expanded in other directions and use technical utilities not limited to one country or region. It is much more costly and time consuming to network different systems and make them cooperate, than to start with one system, centralize all resources and then, depending on user information needs and differing vendor functional connections, decentralize it.

Funding of WAN and Future Plans

Financing WANs and applications on them is becoming more and more the central issue regarding their future development. If statements such as: "In the 1980s, higher education in the United States has managed to keep up with the computer age without an overall plan . . . this will not do in the 1990s,"[15] are true even for the United States, how can we expect that networking in other countries will differ? Most of the WANs in Slovenia were financed by money gained from research contracts. The above-mentioned YSTIS was the only exception—the only project which received money purposely for networking.

In theory, all messages transmitted over the WAN should be related to research and education. In practice, sometimes the only relationship the information has to these areas is that someone working at an educational or research site is sending or receiving it. This could become an equity issue. The Ministry for Science and Technology has allocated money for enhancing library automation through WAN. It is a condition of the grant that the databases which are the output of a library or information center would eventually be available to users through WAN. Some institutions were asked to do the same with databases which they receive from other sources and make licensing agreements with the original database suppliers. The connection between the availability of grants and network accessibility of databases is practiced in other countries, like Great Britain,[16] and usually works positively towards library WAN development.

Financing Structures Based on Library Contribution

We have also considered connecting the financing of libraries with the amount and quality of information they offer on networks. The idea was that when you provide as much information as is found in an OPAC on a WAN, financing should be different from that of an institution of similar size that makes no information available to the network community.[17] But that kind of thinking, although it could expand the quality of library WAN use, is yet to become part of the libraries' financing policies. Libraries can take a leadership role in shaping the future when information dissemination in digital form will be preeminent.[18] All projects underway should help to further coordinate library services of WANs and to exploit their potential through publicity, documentation, and training. Only one bibliographic vendor has been financed at this time, so the spread of local systems, coupled with the existence of more than one bibliographic vendor, may not inhibit successful data exchange and national-level resource sharing, as experienced elsewhere.[19] But how the existence of only one vendor influences development is yet to be seen.

Improving the Communications Infrastructure

A common network bottleneck is slow communications lines that make some services very sluggish, especially during peak hours. So, major efforts will be focused on establishing fast communications lines among key computers in the academic community. Most of the money for this project will be provided by the Ministry of Science and Technology.

At the beginning of 1991, a project was launched to install needed fiber optics required to take advantage of the national networks. Governmental money could help universities and research institutes in their efforts to install fiber-optic networks. War and other economic troubles have stalled this project. Some remnants of fiber optics are present, but the project is waiting for conditions to improve. Unfortunately, we cannot expect full support by the politicians and public in Slovenia, as they do not as yet believe that the government has an obligation to address the equity issue in widespread computer networks. But we can count on some government bodies, especially on the Ministry for Science and Technology.

So, the project is still at its starting phase. The backbone will be a 100MB FDDI (Fiber Distributed Data Interface) link, which will connect seven computers with others connected by Ethernet and terminal links (see Figure 1). These facilities will provide a good base for improving the existing applications, broadening their use, and for adding new applications. One important benefit will be Local Area Vax Cluster software which will closely tie computers through fiber links, enabling effective resource sharing and higher reliability.

How it should work can be seen by plans we have at the Medical Faculty. The central computer at the Medical Faculty (see Figure 2), located at the Institute of Biomedical Informatics (IBMI), will be a node on the network's backbone. We have to provide a means for users to reach the network. In addition to dial-up modem connections which are used today we will have to establish fast fiber-optic links. The first step was to provide such links to the Central Medical Library which has been using them since 1990. Other parts of the Medical Faculty are located rather far from the central computer

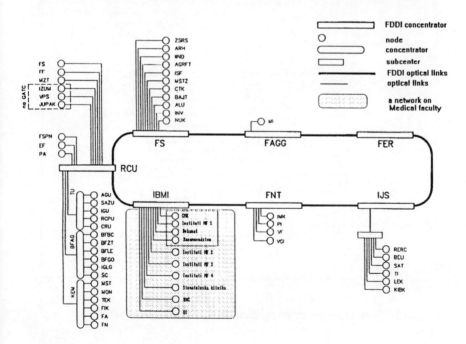

Figure 1. Topology of a network.

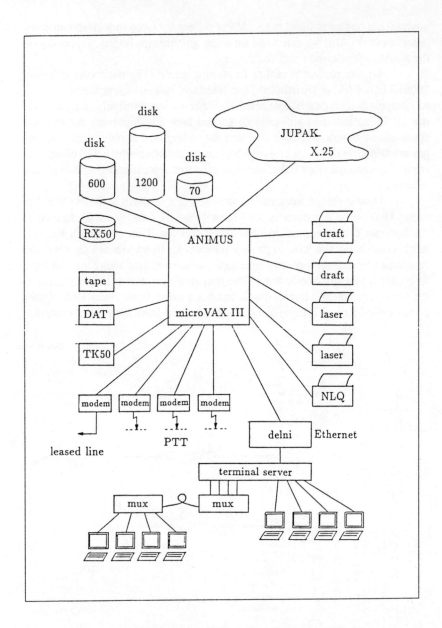

Figure 2. Central computer on medical faculty and its peripherals.

and their integration will be more complicated. However, much work has been done on the project and we hope that we will receive the money for its implementation soon.

Integration of the WAN and Other Information Media

On IBMI some work has been done to integrate compact discs (CD-ROM) to multi-user computers. Now due to limited financial resources we have implemented simple integration through LANs. One computer in a network serves as a gateway to the VAX and enables one terminal user at a time to use services for accessing compact discs. In the future we would like to offer services which will support many fast simultaneous connections.

IBMI has paid considerable attention to the education of potential users of the WAN and others who already use its services. Students receive basic information on the WAN and the Central Medical Library in the first year of their studies. All interested medical students—and these numbers are growing from year to year—can have user names and use these networks. Seminars are also held on the postgraduate level, and special courses are offered to users who want more information. Information about library network services and other online databases are a basic part of these seminars. Seminars are also helping us to see and understand user needs and promote the possibilities of computer networks.[20]

References

1. Cerf, V. 1991. Networks. *Scientific American* 265 (3): 42-51.

2. Avram, H. 1988. Toward a Nationwide Library Network. *Journal of Library Administration* 8 (3/4): 95-116.

3. Gherman, P. 1988. Vision and Reality: The Research Libraries and Networking. *Journal of Library Administration* 8 (3/4): 51-57.

4. Arms, C. 1990. Using the National Networks: BITNET and the Internet. *Online* 14 (5): 24-29.

5. Zebec, B., and T. Seljak. 1990. Libraries and Information Centres Within Yugoslav Scientific and Technological Information (YSTIS). *European Conference on Library Automation and Networking.* K. G. Saur Muenchen.

6. Popovic, M. 1991. . . . Yugoslavia . . . *Journal of Documentation* 47 (2): 199-203.

7. Heningman, B. 1991. Networking and Authority Control: Online Catalog Authority Control in Illinois. *Information Technology and Libraries* 3: 47-54.

8. Adamic, S. 1990. SBMNI: devet godina od ideje (Nine Years Since the Idea). *Periodicum Biologorum* 92 (2): 205-209.

9. Kalin, S., and R. Tennant. 1991. Beyond OPACs. . .The Wealth for Information Resources on the Internet. *Database* 8: 28-33.

10. Juznic, P. 1991. Interlibrary Lending in Yugoslavia: With Special Reference to the Central Medical Library in Ljubljana. *Interlending and Document Supply* 19 (3): 94-100.

11. Alberico, R. 1990. The Development of an "Information Superhighway." *Computers in Libraries* 1: 33-35.

12. Dickman, S. 1990. Eastern Europe Comes Online. *Nature* 348: 378.

13. Riggs, D. 1988. Networking and Institutional Planning. *Journal of Library Administration* 8 (3/4): 59-67.

14. Lowry, C. 1988. Ownership of Bibliographic Data and Its Importance to Consortia. *Journal of Library Administration* 8 (3/4): 69-84.

15. Atkinson, R. 1990. Wiring the Campuses. *Science* 248 (4955): 529.

16. Buxton, A. 1988. JANET and the Librarian. *Electronic Library* 6 (4): 250-263.

17. Buckland, M., and C. Lynch. 1987. The Linked Systems Protocol and the Future of Bibliographic Networks and Systems. *Information Technology and Libraries* 6: 83-88.

18. Cisler, S. 1991. NREN Update: More Meetings and New Tools. *Database* 4: 96-98.

19. Flanders, B. 1991. NREN: The Big Issues Aren't Technical. *American Libraries* 22 (6): 572-575.

20. Hudomalj, E. 1991. Akademska ra~unalni{ka omre 'ja in njihov pomen v biomedicini (Academic Networks and Their Role in Biomedicine). *Zdravstveni vestnik* 60 (30): 131-134.

Glossary

ARPA (Advanced Research Projects Agency). An agency of the U.S. Defense Department that began ARPANET in 1969.

ARPANET. Packet-switched network started in 1969 by government funds of ARPA (Advanced Research Projects Agency).

ASCII (American Standard Code for Information Interchange, pronounced "ask-ee"). A commonly used coding scheme used to represent computer-generated information.

ATM (Asynchronous Transfer Mode). A true cell (fixed length) relay network system that represents a fundamental change in network conceptualization with transmission speeds reaching 600mbps.

BITNET (Because It's Time NETwork). Began in 1981 as a inexpensive, rather slow international network for educational and research institutions that is often used for e-mail type messages, and in 1989 merged into CREN (The Corporation for Research and Educational Networking).

bps (bits per second). A measurement of the rate of transmission with speeds of 2,400, 9,600, and 19,200bps being common rates of speed for modem transmissions connected to networks via regular telephone lines. Transmission speeds over networks are often measured in units of thousands, kbps (kilobits per second) as well as units of millions, mbps (millions of bits per second). Using a modem transmission rate of 2,400 bps an average 200-page book (text) would be sent in approximately 22 minutes, a LAN might transmit at 2.5mbps so the same book would be transmitted in less than one second, and a fiber-optic cable network may reach speeds of 100mbps, in which case a 200-page book might be sent in less than one twenty-fifth of a second.

Bridge. A hardware device with software that connects and forwards packets of information among two or more networks which have the same network operating system, but need not have the same hardware systems and protocol. That is to say, a bridge can connect the widely-used Ethernet system with ARCNET, another hardware protocol system.

Brouter. A hardware device that combines the features of the bridge and the router technologies that provides fast connections among networks with different protocols.

CCTTT (Consultative Committee on International Telegraph and Telephone from the French, Comité Consulatif International Télégraphique et Téléphonique). An international organization that strives for international agreement on protocols for telecommunications and data transmission standards such as the X.25 network protocol, X.29, and V.32. See X.25, X.29, and V.32.

COSINE (Cooperation for Open Systems Interconnection Networking in Europe). An important pan-European cooperative to network all of greater Europe, funded by European countries and CEC (Commission of the European Communities). IXI as the telecommunications backbone is a major project of COSINE. See IXI.

CREN (The Corporation for Research and Educational Networking, pronounced "kren"). This organization is the September 1989 combination of BITNET (Because It's Time Network) and CSNET (Computer Science NETwork).

DDSs (Digital Data Services). Communications services that provide digital private lines of speeds from 2.4 to 56kbps. Originally, DDS referred to AT&T's Digital Dataphone Service.

DSU/CSU (Data Service Unit/Channel Service Unit). A hardware device that interfaces between the computer and the digital signals of the network. It replaces the computer/modem interface which handles the common analog communications along regular phone lines.

Enterprise network. A network of computers, often PCs, that interconnects the geographically dispersed locations of a corporation and shares vital business information.

Ethernet. A commonly used LAN hardware protocol originally developed by Xerox Corporation that allows network nodes to transmit packets any time over coaxial, twisted-pair, and fiber-optic cabling.

FDDI (Fiber Distributed Data Interface). A proposed standard by the American National Standards Institute (ANSI) for high-speed transmissions of 100mbps using fiber-optic lines.

Fiber optic. A transmission line (cable) made of glass threads which permits signals to be sent very fast by using light as the sending medium.

File server. A large, fast hard disk drive, often a microcomputer (80386 or 80486 model), that interacts and shares information with other micro-computers within a network. In large networks mini and mainframe computers can act as file servers.

Fractional T-1. A communications subset of the T-1 channel. FT-1 is less expensive (lower charge rate) than T-1 because only a portion of the bandwidth is used at any one time. Interexchange carriers sell fractional T1 service commonly at rates of 384, 512, and 768kbps.

Fractional T-3. A communications system of lines similar to T-3 that uses portions of the bandwidth at speeds of 44.7mbps.

Frame relay. Blocks of data of varying lengths called frames sent (relayed) across a packet-switched network at high speeds. Frame relay requires clean transmission lines, as the simplified packets do not contain error correction, flow control, or sequencing information as is the case for X.25 packets.

FTP (File Transfer Protocol). A protocol that allows users to transfer files electronically from remote, off-site computers back to the user's computer without regard to the hardware or operating systems involved. It is part of the TCP/IP/TELENET software suite.

Gateway. Hardware device and accompanying software that allow telecommunications between two or more networks that may have dissimilar protocols and operating systems.

Internet. A network of networks that is international in membership, uses the same telecommunications protocol TCP/IP (Transmission Control Protocol/Internet Protocol) and is predominantly an e-mail and file transfer system.

ISDN (Integrated Services Digital Network). An international standard proposed by CCITT for network-to-network communications that combines voice and data in all digital transmissions at rates of 144kbps to 2mbps. It is currently available only in major U.S. cities, but more commonly found in Asia and Europe.

IXI. An X.25-based network that carries X.29 interactive transmissions and X.400 electronic mail.

kbps (kilo bits per second). See bps.

LAN. See Local-area network.

leased line. A communications line usually supplied by a telephone company that is reserved (dedicated) for permanent use. Also called private line.

LISTSERV software. Software originally developed by IBM for BITNET that manages electronic communications by electronic mail over BITNET/ Internet using LISTSERV protocols. Users subscribe and unsubscribe themselves to various user and discussion groups.

Local-area network. A grouping of two or more computers, often personal computers, that are connected through hardware and software in order to share information within a limited physical space.

MAN. See Metropolitan-area network.

mbps (millions of bits per second). See bps.

Metropolitan-area network. A voice and computer-based public network that covers the area of a city and environs (typically over a range of 25 to 50 miles, 40 to 80 km.) and often uses fiber optic and coaxial lines for very high-speed, error-free transmissions.

MIME (Multipurpose Internet Mail Extension). A proposed standard that addresses the transmission needs of the emerging multimedia communications among networks.

NFSNET (National Science Foundation Network). NSF is a government agency that funds the development and expansion of the U.S.-wide telecommunications backbone for networks called NFSNET. This electronic super-highway includes major universities and their supercomputers.

NREN (National Research and Education Network). Under the management of NSF (National Science Foundation) this network will provide high-speed interconnections between national and regional networks.

OPAC (online public access catalog). OPACs are one of the promises of a nation-wide access and sharing of resources among libraries. See Z39.50.

OSI (Open Systems Interconnection) model. An international standard for the protocol of transmission and interconnection which is organized into seven conceptual and hierarchical layers.

Packet. A unit of information (data) that is sent or received over networks.

PAD (Packet assembler/disassembler). A combination of hardware and software that allows an interface between an X.25 network and an asynchronous device such as a typical PC modem.

PBX (Private Branch eXchange). The common telephone switching system for both internal and external calling.

PDNs (Public Data Networks). The long-distance telephone companies that offer network telecommunications services. Also called VANs (Value-Added Networks).

Protocol. A formal set of rules that governs various aspects of communications (such as data format, timing of message exchange, error handling) between network nodes.

Repeater. A hardware device that amplifies and retransmits signals so that the transmission can be sent a longer distance.

Router. A hardware device that chooses the best path to send a transmission packet with greater security and less speed than a bridge.

SMDS (Switched Multimegabit Data Service). A cell (fixed length) relay network system that is projected to send transmissions up to speeds of 45mbps. Developed by Bell Telecommunications Research, it provides for faster, more economical transmissions, as compared to an X.25 network.

SMTP (Simple Mail Transfer Protocol). An electronic mail (e-mail) protocol commonly used in TCP/IP networks. SMTP provides a common specification for exchange of electronic mail messages between two mail systems.

T-1. A 1.544mbps communications circuit of private, digital lines that provides transmission of voice, video, and data and is typically divided into twenty-four 64kbps. T-1 is a leased-line service that is found about everywhere in the United States.

T-3. A digital communications system typically delivered over fiber-optic cable that provides transmission up to speeds of 44.736mbps, supporting 28 T-1 channels.

TCP/IP (Transmission Control Protocol/Internet Protocol). A suite of communications protocols standardized by the U.S. Department of Defense and used by the Internet network. IP receives the data from TCP, breaks the data into packets and then ships it off to a network within the Internet. TCP/IP is gaining in use and popularity over OSI and is the de facto standard (as of 1992) for internetworking.

UUCP (Unix to Unix Copy Program). An application program that allows UNIX systems to copy and share files and refers to UNIX electronic mail transfer.

V.32 (v dot 32). A modem standard that allows data rates of 9,600bps that can transmit over ordinary two-wire, dial-up telephone lines. V.32 modems are commonly manufactured with built-in data compression or error-correction features.

V.42. A CCITT standard for modem error correction, and the V.42bis is for data compression. VANs (Value-Added Networks) see PDNs.

WAIS (wide-area information servers). As the concept of a nation-wide data network evolves, the experimental WAIS system represents a collaborative experimental research project to develop a vast computer library which would provide a user-friendly format for users to search volumes of information via the Internet network.

Wide-area network (WAN). A network of computers, often PCs in the library setting, that covers a very large geographical area. Often times, groups of LANs are tied together to form a WAN system.

X.25. X dot 25 is the current international CCITT WAN digital communications hardware protocol that provides packet switching. The protocol specifies standards for assembly of data streams into packets, the packet's control, routing, and protection during their migration over the network.

X.29. CCITT standard for communications exchange of information between a local PAD and a remote PAD. See PAD.

X.400. The CCITT protocol for electronic mail (e-mail).

X.500. A protocol for directories (listing) that names users in WANs.

X.PC protocol. A protocol developed by Tymnet that improves the interface of microcomputers to the PC connection to its X.25 network.

X-Windows system. An MIT-developed software system that manages output on bitmapped displays. Rectangular areas (windows) of graphics or texts are displayed on the monitor screen and can be created, enlarged, overlapped, and erased by a program titled "window manager."

Z39.50 protocol. National standard developed by the National Information Standards Organization (NISO) that defines an applications level protocol by which one computer can query another computer and transfer records. This protocol is the framework for an OPAC (online public access catalog) user to search off-site catalogs on Internet. SR (Search and Retrieval) is the international version of Z39.50.

Contributors

Bruce Flanders holds a B.A. from the University of Kansas and an M.S. from the University of Illinois. He is the director of technology for the Kansas State Library, where he administers the Kansas Library Catalog and KIC-NET, the interlibrary loan telecommunications network described in this book. He is a guest lecturer for the School of Library and Information Management, Emporia (Kansas) State University, where he has taught courses in introductory and advanced cataloging. He is a contributing editor and monthly columnist for *American Libraries*, and has written numerous articles for Meckler journals, including *CD-ROM Librarian, Computers in Libraries, Electronic Networking: Research, Applications, and Policies* and *Research & Education Networking*.

Bruce Flanders
Director of Technology
Kansas State Library
Capitol Building, Rm. 343N
Topeka, KS 66612-1593

voice: 913-296-3296
fax: 913-296-6650
e-mail: FLANDERS@UKANVM.BITNET
flanders@ukanvm.cc.ukans.edu

Henry (Hank) Harken has been the electronic information specialist at the Fletcher Library of Arizona State University West in Phoenix, Arizona, since 1986. His responsibilities include all aspects of technology as it affects the mission of the Fletcher Library, including microcomputing hardware and software, CD-ROM, networking, and telecommunications. He also administers the library's local-area network of over forty computers and other devices. He is a contributor to *Library LANs: Case Studies in Practice and Application* (Meckler, 1992), and is a frequent speaker at annual and mid-year meetings of the Arizona State Library Association and other conferences in the United States. He held the position of coordinator for online searching at the Margaret I. King Library while at the University of Kentucky, 1982-1986, and was newsletter editor of the Central/Eastern Kentucky Online Users Group. He previously worked at Tennessee Technological University in Cookeville, Tennessee, and at King Faisal University in Saudi Arabia.

Henry (Hank) Harken
Fletcher Library
Arizona State University West
P.O. Box 37100
Phoenix, AZ 85069

voice: 602-543-8507
fax: 602-543-8521
e-mail: IADHRH@ASUACAD.BITNET

Emil Hudomalj holds a B.S. in electrical engineering from the University of Ljubljana (Slovenia). He worked on image processing there as a research fellow in the Laboratory for Artificial Intelligence and Process Information Systems. He is currently an assistant professor at the Medical Faculty, University of Ljubljana. His latest research and professional work deals with computer networks, image processing, and computer vision. He is an active member of the Slovene Biomedical Information Association.

Emil Hudomalj
Institute for Biomedical Informatics
Medical Faculty / University of Ljubljana
Vrazov trg 2
YU-61105 Ljubljana
Slovenia

voice: +38 61 310 732
fax: +38 61 311 540
e-mail: emil.hudomalj@uni-LJ.ac.mail.yu

Ann-Sofi Israelson holds an M.A. from Linköping University and a M. Libr. Sc. from Boras. She has worked as librarian in the University and the Geotechnical Institute in Linköping, and as head of public services and collections in the Royal Institute of Technology Library, Stockholm, before joining the Organisation Européenne pour la Recherche Nucléaire (European Organization for Nuclear Research, or CERN), Geneva, in 1988 as deputy head of Scientific Information Services.

Ann-Sofi Israelson
CERN (European Organization for Nuclear Research)
CH-1211 Geneva 23
Switzerland

voice: +41-22-7674966
e-mail: israels@cernvm. cern.ch

Primoz Juznic is the chief librarian at the Central Medical Library, Medical Faculty, University of Ljbuljana (Slovenia), and an assistant professor at the Medical Faculty. Among his previous posts are the chief librarian at the Central Library for Social Sciences and the head of the Department of Planning and Development at the Research Council of Slovenia. Besides being an active member of the Slovene Union of Librarians and the Biomedical Information Association, he is a member of the European Assocation for Health Information and Libraries, and the European Library Automation Group. His latest research and professional work, and published manuscripts deal with interlibrary loan services and union catalogs, integration of the library community into wide-area networks and OPACs.

Primoz Juznic
Central Medical Library
Medical Faculty / University of Ljubljana
Vrazov trg 2
YU-61105 Ljubljana
Slovenia

voice: +38 61 310 732
fax: +38 61 311 540
e-mail: primoz.juznic@uni-lj.ac.mail.yu

Achille Petrilli holds a physics diploma from the University of Bologna (Italy). He has been working in CERN since 1983, responsible first for workstation operations and then for the installation and operations of a Cray supercomputer. He is currently deputy head of the Management Information Services.

Achille Petrilli
CERN (European Organization for Nuclear Research)
CH-1211 Geneva 23
Switzerland

voice: +41-22-7678136
e-mail: petrilli@cernvm.cern.ch

Mogens Sandfaer graduated from the Royal Danish School of Librarianship in 1981. He has worked on the Danish National Bibliography, in the Danish Institute for Marine Research (chief librarian) and in the Danish National Library of Technology (head of computer systems), before joining the Scientific Information Services in CERN, Geneva, in 1990 as head of systems development and maintenance.

Mogens Sandfaer
CERN (European Organization for Nuclear Research)
CH-1211 Geneva 23
Switzerland

voice: +41-22-7672372
e-mail: sand@cernvm.cern.ch

Stephan Schwarz received his Ph.D. in physics from Stockholm University. He had been working for the Swedish National Institute for Defence Research, OECD Nuclear Energy Agency (Paris), and the Royal Institute of Technology (as university librarian 1973-87) before joining CERN, Geneva, as head of Scientific Information Services. He has traveled extensively in Eastern Africa, Southeast Asia and China, and Central America as a consultant for UNESCO.

Stephan Schwarz
CERN (European Organization for Nuclear Research)
CH-1211 Geneva 23
Switzerland

voice: +41-22-7672454
e-mail: schwarz@cernvm.cern.ch

Len Simutis holds an A.B. in English from the University of Illinois, and an M.A. and Ph.D. in American Studies from the University of Minnesota. He is executive director of the Ohio Library and Information Network (Ohio-LINK). Prior to joining OhioLINK in 1990, he served as dean of the Graduate School and Research, and special assistant to the Provost for Academic Information Systems at Miami University, Oxford, Ohio, from 1984-90. He also served as a member of the faculty, chair of the Division of Environmental and Urban Studies, and assistant and associate dean in the College of Architecture and Urban Studies at Virginia Tech from 1971-84. He has done teaching and research on geographic information systems and environmental planning, and is a consultant on high-voltage transmission line location for Appalachian Power and American Electric Power. He is also a member of the Ohio Humanities Council. His current research interests include the development of scholarly information systems and the use of advanced workstation technology for information retrieval and analysis.

Len Simutis
Executive Director
Ohio Library and Information Network
1224 Kinnear Road
Columbus, OH 43212

voice: 614-292-0067
fax: 614-292-7168
e-mail: len@ohiolink.edu

Peter Stone is sub-librarian for Information Services at the University of Sussex, at Brighton on the south coast of England. He has worked there happily for over twenty years, largely on the management and implementation of library systems. Actively involved in the development of information services and library use of JANET, he has been a member of many of the project groups and committees. His report for the British Library, *JANET: A Report on Its Use for Libraries*, was published in 1990.

Peter Stone
University of Sussex Library
Brighton, BN1 9QL
United Kingdom

voice: +44 273 678475
fax: +44 273 678441
e-mail: p.t.stone@central.sussex.ac.uk

Gregory Zuck holds an M.L.S. from Indiana University-Bloomington and a Ph.D. from the University of Wisconsin-Madison. He is library director of Southwestern College, and an active member of the Library Information and Technology Association (LITA) as chairperson of interest groups in Desktop publishing, e-mail/electronic bulletin boards, and is founder of the Small Library Integrated Systems Interest Group. He has given programs at many American Library Association (ALA) conferences, and is chair of the Kansas

Automation and Technology Roundtable. He has been a faculty member at the library schools of the University of Oregon, North Texas State University, and the University of Iowa. His current interests are in microcomputer-based library applications, telecommunications, and small system automation.

Gregory Zuck
Library Director
Southwestern College
100 College Street
Winfield, KS 67156

voice: 316-221-4150
fax: 316-221-3725

Index